OFF-OFF BROADWAY FESTIVAL PLAYS
EIGHTEENTH SERIES

Selected by New York theatre critics, professionals, and the editorial staff of Samuel French, Inc. as the most important plays in the Eighteenth Annual Off-Off-Broadway Original Short Play Festival, sponsored by Love Creek Productions.

LAST EXIT BEFORE TOLL
by Carrie Goldstein

PEACE IN OUR TIME
by Larry Cadman

SOMETHING ROTTEN IN DENMARK
by Annie G.

HOW MANY TO TANGO?
by Sandra J. Albert

VISITING OLIVER
by Bill Nave

THE POWER AND THE GLORY
by Le Wilhelm

JUST THINKING
by Alan H. Kravitz

PASQUINI THE MAGNIFICENT
by Sam Ingraffia

SAMUEL FRENCH, INC.

45 West 25th Street   New York, 10010-2751
7623 Sunset Blvd.   Hollywood 90046-2795

IMPORTANT BILLING AND CREDIT
REQUIREMENTS

All producers of LAST EXIT BEFORE TOLL, PEACE IN OUR TIME, SOMETHING ROTTEN IN DENMARK, HOW MANY TO TANGO?, VISITING OLIVER, THE POWER AND THE GLORY, JUST THINKING and PASQUINI THE MAGNIFICENT *must* give credit to the Author(s) of the Play(s) in all programs distributed in connection with performances of the Play(s) and in all instances in which the title(s) of the Play appear(s) for purposes of advertising, publicizing or otherwise exploiting the Play(s) and/or a production. The name of the Author *must* also appear on a separate line, on which no other name appears, immediately following the title, and *must* appear in size of type not less than fifty percent the size of the title type.

TABLE OF CONTENTS

LAST EXIT BEFORE TOLL 7

PEACE IN OUR TIME..17

SOMETHING ROTTEN IN DENMARK 33

HOW MANY TO TANGO?......................................59

VISITING OLIVER..81

THE POWER AND THE GLORY 105

JUST THINKING 117

PASQUINI THE MAGNIFICENT...........................147

LAST EXIT BEFORE TOLL

A Telephone Monologue

by Carrie Goldstein

LAST EXIT BEFORE TOLL was presented by Quaigh Theatre and directed by Will Lieberson with the following cast:

WOMAN ....Sara Lowell

Sets/Lights/Sound by Ralph Thornton
Stage Management by Paul Brandt

CHARACTERS

WOMAN

TIME & PLACE

Present. Suburbia, USA

LAST EXIT BEFORE TOLL

A suburban housewife answers her RINGING telephone.

Hello.

Oh hi, honey. How's the office?

Good. Good.

Oh yeah. I had a nice day. I went to see Millie.

Millie.

You know Millie. The one that lived in 3G whose husband is in poultry products with blackheads.

Millie. With the legs.

Yes. That Millie.

No. She lives in Westchester now. She bought a ranch.

Well she wanted a good school district. Her oldest one is in this special program where you don't learn until you ask. I don't know. You'd think she'd be worried. He's in third grade and he can't write his name because he never asked.

Well, to each his own. Look, speaking of kids, could you do me a favor on the way home?

No. It's right on your way.

Well, when you get to the toll booth at the Throgs Neck Bridge go through the toll all the way on the right.

No, it's not an exact change.

Yeah, maybe it'll take two minutes longer, but I'm sure the car pool will understand if you explain.

Well, this morning when I left for Millie's I took my brown pocketbook. You know where my money was? In my multicolored. In my whole life I never walked out the door without money. So I was about to come home to get it, but then I found enough quarters in the door handle thing, you know, so I could pay on the bridge to get to Millie's and I figured I'll borrow some money from her to get back home. Well, I don't know what I was thinking when I left there, but I forgot. Can you believe that? So when I passed the sign that says "Last Exit Before Toll" I didn't know what I was going to do. But then I figure, what am I worrying. It's not like it's a whole lot of money. They'll see I'm good for it. After all, I'm driving an Oldsmobile and they'll tell me when it's convenient I should come and pay it. So I pull all the way over on the right so I wouldn't block any traffic and this guy comes over and I tell him what happened. So he goes over to talk to some other guy and they both stand there looking at me and talking and then they call over a third guy and then the first one goes into this building there, like an office or something and he comes out and he starts filling out these papers and then he comes back to me and he looks at my license and my registration and he asks me where am I going and where am I coming from and the other two guys are still standing there talking and looking over at me and then this first guy gives me this pink form to sign that I swear I'll mail in the money within thirty days under penalty of law and I sign it and then he says, "Wait here a minute" and he goes back and talks to the other guys again and he comes back with the third guy that came and he looks in at me like I'm some sort of criminal and he asks me, "Do I understand what I signed?" and I said "Of course I understand what I signed", and I was really beginning to feel like I was an outlaw or something, like what did he think, I'm going to get rich by cheating the toll booth people, like I have nothing better to do, but I didn't say it. I was really polite and I kept saying I was sorry and he says, "Just so you understand this money's got to be paid in thirty days" and I said, "I'll mail it the minute I get home" and he says "O.K. You can go now" and he opens up this gate to let me through and I turn on the motor and I start pulling up and I see, in the mirror, the first two guys, they're still looking at the car and it made me feel really funny that they would think I was trying to get away with something so I put the car in reverse and I back up and I roll down the window and I say to the second guy, "Look, what makes you think I'm trying to get away with something? I told you I'd send in the money" and he said "I know" and I said "Well nobody's acting like they know" and he said "We believe you lady" and I said "Look, just to prove that I'm not trying to cheat you I'm going to leave you some collateral and that way you'll really believe I'm honest and when I pay the money you'll give me my collateral back." So he said "O.K." and I gave him the baby.

Our baby.

Well of course, I know it was dumb, but at the time it seemed like the only way to prove I wasn't trying to cheat them.

No. He didn't seem to mind. And the baby didn't. You know how friendly he is. He goes to anybody. Anyway, the guy's name is Vince, so when you go over the Throgs Neck just go on the right, ask for Vince, give him the toll money and he'll give you the baby.

Good. I'll call him and tell him you're coming. See you soon.

Pot roast.

Bye.

(SHE telephones.)

Hello. Is this the toll booth area?

Is Vince there?

Hello Vince?

This is the lady in the Oldsmobile that didn't have the money.

Right. Listen, I wanted to tell you I didn't mail it in yet because I figured out a way you wouldn't have to wait for it. My husband's going to stop by on his way home and pay it.

Yeah, I thought you'd think so. So he'll give you the money and you'll rip up that pink form I signed.

You mean you have to file it?

Well just so you mark it down that it's paid.

Good. How's Mark?

Mark — the baby.

I didn't tell you his name? It's Mark.

Oh, isn't that cute. Yeah, he loves to play with keys.

That's adorable. All right, so my husband will be there soon and you'll give him the baby and we'll be even.

O.K. Bye.

BLACKOUT

(SHE telephones.)

Hello. I'd like to talk to Vince please.

Yeah, I'll hold.

Hello, Vince? This is the lady from yesterday. You know, I didn't have the money?

Yeah, listen. Now you probably really think I'm trying to cheat you but, it's just — well, my husband just couldn't get there yesterday.

Well, there's this guy in his car pool who's always in a rush and he wanted to take the Whitestone.

Well he was driving so he had his choice of routes, but tonight my husband's driving so for sure he'll be there. Look, Vince, tell him what he owes you for Pampers.

No. I wouldn't worry about that. Try giving him a little strained apricots.

O.K. Vince. So you'll get my toll money tonight.

Fine. Bye.

BLACKOUT

(SHE telephones.)

Hello. Is Vince there?

Oh, Vince. I didn't recognize your voice. You don't usually answer.

This is the lady, remember a few weeks ago, I didn't have the money for the toll and ...

Right. Mark's mother. How are you?

Good. Look, I'm really embarrassed but, well my husband doesn't come home over your bridge anymore.

Well it turned out the Whitestone was faster. And well, I just haven't been able to get out of the house.

Well, I'm getting this sort of like string wallpaper in the dining room and new tile in the downstairs bathroom and the painters are in and you've just got to be here to watch them every minute.

That's right. You pay for the expensive paint and they sneak in the cheap stuff on you. Anyway, look, they're going to be finished here on Wednesday. Thursday I have an appointment with the periodontist ...

Gums. So he's going to do a lot of work on me on Thursday and he said I should expect a lot of pain. But Friday, if I'm feeling good, I'll come and pay my money and — you're keeping track of what you're spending on Mark, I hope.

Really? You got him a flu shot? Did he have a reaction?

That's not so bad. So you gave him a little baby aspirin?

Good. Then I'll see you on Friday.

BLACKOUT

(SHE telephones.)

I'd like to talk to Vince, please.

Hi, Vince. This is the lady who — well it's more than a year now, but remember the toll? You know, Mark's mother.

Yeah. How's everything?

Look, I know I promised you, but I just haven't been able to get there.

Well, I've just been so busy, and now, I'm really tied down. I just had a new baby.

A boy. He looks just like Mark. Maybe Mark was a little lighter, but they really look like brothers. You couldn't mistake them.

Brian David.

Seven - two.

Yeah, it's a good size. Look Vince, just as soon as I get this baby off formula, I'll be there to settle up with you.

BLACKOUT

(SHE telephones.)

Hello, Vince?

That's right. How'd you know?

You're really good at voices, because Brian's in first grade already so it must be ...

Oh yeah, he loves it. He gets smile faces every day.

Smile faces. Mark never got a smile face?

For good work.

Well that's the same thing. Some teachers give smile faces. Some teachers give stars. So he gets a lot of stars, huh?

Good for him. You know, Vince, like I said, Brian's in first grade, but he's still a baby in a lot of things and I really think if I all of a sudden tell him he's got a brother it could do a lot of damage.

That's what I mean. Psychologically. So, if it's all right with you, I'm going to wait 'til he's a little bit older.

BLACKOUT

(SHE telephones.)

Hello, Vince?

Vince — er — I don't know his last name.

Well yes, it's been a long time ...

Yes, that's the one.

He's in Florida? Oh, on vacation, I guess.

What do you mean he's retired? How could he be retired?

Well look, someone there must have his phone number or something.

You do? Well, then ...

Oh, but I'm sure he won't mind if I have it.

Well, all right. You check it out and I'll call you back. Just let me write down who I should ask for.

Is that Mark with a "c" or a "k"?

BLACKOUT

END OF PLAY

Author's Note

It is with pleasure that I suggest that the director and production staff use whatever sets, staging, costumes, and props seem appropriate. Often they will have ideas far more imaginative than mine. The words, however, are immutable.

Carrie Goldstein

Carrie Goldstein (nee Schillin) was born and raised in Brooklyn, New York. She attended first, Brooklyn College, and then City College and was awarded a Bachelor's degree in American and English Literature. More recently she earned a master's degree in Computer Science from the New York Institute of Technology.

She also studied at BMI's Musical Theatre Workshop and wrote the libretti for several children's musical stage productions. Among these are *Rumplestiltskin*, *Beauty and the Beast*, and *David*. Non-musical productions in New York City include *Golden Links* and *Lifestyle*.

She presently lives in Glen Cove, New York.

PEACE IN OUR TIME

by Larry Cadman

Peace in Our Time was presented by Playmarket. It was directed by Alyce Mott with the following cast:

PETE ....Darrel Adleman

ERIC ....William Ellis

CHARACTERS

PETE

ERIC

TIME & PLACE

A park bench near the Vietnam Memorial in Washington D.C.

PEACE IN OUR TIME

A park bench near the Vietnam Memorial in Washington D.C. The Memorial Wall itself is offstage right. Throughout the play, the characters will look in that direction when referring to it. A MAN is seated on the bench. HE is in his forties, dressed in a well-tailored business suit. HE is taking pictures of the monument with a 35mm SLR camera. A second MAN enters from stage right. HE, too, is in his forties. HE is dressed in jeans and an old army fatigue shirt. HE is carrying an army surplus canvas bag. In contrast to the first man, HE has a wild and seedy look

ERIC. Don't take our picture, man.
PETE. Excuse me?
ERIC. I said, don't take our picture. I don't like it.
PETE. I was taking a picture of the memorial.

(ERIC sits down on the bench.)

ERIC. I'm in that picture.
PETE. I was taking a picture of the memorial. There are people standing next to the memorial. Maybe one of them was you. How should I know? What's the big deal?

(ERIC unzips his canvas bag and takes out a huge hero sandwich. HE takes a quick, savage bite.)

ERIC. No big deal. I just don't like it.
PETE. When I get the pictures developed, and I see the one with you in it, I'll throw it away. Okay? Will that satisfy you?
ERIC. Guess it'll have to. Want a piece?
PETE. No, thank you. (*HE takes another picture of the memorial.*)

19

ERIC. I'm curious, man. Why are taking pictures of that? You gonna carry them around in your wallet or something?

PETE. It's an historic monument.

ERIC. It ain't a historic monument, man. It's a goddamn public pacifier. I mean, look at them people. They come from all over, and they stand there, and they look at the names, and they feel like shit for a couple of minutes, then they go to lunch and have a nice crab salad sandwich. It's a pacifier, man. It's bull shit.

PETE. I don't think it's bull shit.

ERIC. Take your pictures now, man. They could be more historic than you think.

PETE. Excuse me. I'm just going over here to get a different angle. (*HE starts to leave.*)

ERIC. You afraid of me, man? You don't have to be afraid of me.

PETE. (*Stops.*) I'm not afraid of you. Why should I be?

ERIC. Yeah. Exactly. Why should you be? I'm just enjoying a quiet day here. Like you.

(*PETE is now unsure whether to stay or go. HE stays.*)

PETE. What did you mean just now? That these pictures could be more historic than I think?

ERIC. I didn't mean nothing. Don't mind me. I just talk sometimes. So, what about it, man? You ever take pictures of living things? You got kids? A wife?

PETE. Yes.

ERIC. You got a second, man? Can I show you something?

PETE. I guess.

(*ERIC reaches inside his jacket and pulls out a wallet. HE rummages through it and extracts a small photograph. HE hands it to the PETE.*)

ERIC. My wife.

PETE. She's ... pretty. Very pretty. Young.

ERIC. It was taken a while ago.

PETE. Do you live around here?

ERIC. We're not together anymore, man. We didn't make it.

PETE. I'm sorry. (*HE hands the picture back.*)

ERIC. So, can I see yours?

PETE. What?

ERIC. Your wife and kids. The pictures.

PETE. Oh. Sure. I guess so.

(*PETE puts his camera down and reaches for his wallet. ERIC grabs the camera and starts taking pictures.*)

ERIC. Smile, man. Say cheese. Watch the birdie. (*HE can't get the camera to operate.*) What's wrong with this thing, man? It don't work.

PETE. Will you please give me the camera back?

ERIC. How's this thing work? I want to take your picture. For your wife and kiddies.

PETE. It's a very complicated piece of equipment. Please give it back. (*HE reaches over and takes the camera out of the Eric's hands.*)

ERIC. It's okay, man. I wasn't going to hurt it. I just wanted to take your picture.

(*PETE examines his camera.*)

ERIC. Is it all right?

PETE. Yes, it's fine.

ERIC. I didn't bust it or nothing?

PETE. No.

ERIC. That's good. I guess if you bust a complicated piece of equipment like that, it's expensive to fix. So, you gonna show me? (*Pause.*) The pictures, man.

(*PETE takes some pictures out of his wallet.*)

ERIC. Your little girl? How old?

PETE. Twelve.

ERIC. She's gonna break some hearts before she's through. Look at that smile. (*HE looks at another picture.*) Your son, man? What's his name?

PETE. Pete. Pete, Jr.

ERIC. Pete? You're kidding. Your name is Pete? Oh, man, what a coincidence. Let me introduce myself. My name is Eric.

(ERIC shakes his hand. HE continues to look at the picture.)

ERIC. You don't let him play with guns, do you?

PETE. I don't get it. What's the coincidence?

ERIC. Say what?

PETE. You said it was a coincidence. That my name is Pete.

ERIC. Yeah. My best friend's name is Pete. I was just talking with him. He's over there. (*ERIC points in the direction of the memorial.*)

PETE. Where?

ERIC. Over there, man. On the wall. Section E36. Peter Thomas Kosmeric. He's dead, man.

PETE. Jesus. You were there.

ERIC. Two tours, Pete. '68 to '70. The vintage years. Hey, Pete, I gotta little riddle for you. Why was the Vietnam War like a rat that chased its own tail?

PETE. I don't know.

ERIC. Well, now, dammit, if you knew your Memorial, Pete, you'd know the answer to that. You see that center panel there, the tallest one? Well, right at the top there is the name of the first man who died in Nam. And at the bottom of the same panel is the name of the last man who died. And in between, going all the way around and back are the names of 58,130 other guys who died so we could end up in the same place we started from. No where. (*Pause.*) Now in terms of years, at the the top there ... you see at the top there? That was the year 1959. When Eisenhower sent in the advisors. Sounds clean and safe, don't it? Being an advisor? 'Cept if you look, there was quite a few guys ended up dead advisors. Guess they followed some bad advice, huh? (*ERIC laughs.*) Just made a little joke, Pete. Laugh. Come on. LAUGH!

PETE. I don't see anything funny about it.

ERIC. (*Mocking Pete's tone.*) "I don't see anything funny about it." You weren't there, were you, man?

PETE. No, I wasn't.

ERIC. How come, man? You and I look about the same age.

PETE. I was deferred.

ERIC. Yeah?

PETE. I was a student.

ERIC. Uh-hm. What'd you study?

PETE. Philosophy.

ERIC. Philosophy? You're shitting me, right?

PETE. No.

ERIC. We knew they were letting guys out for medical school. We never knew they were deferring the philosophers. That's so fucking perfect, man.

PETE. I know it didn't seem fair. It probably wasn't.

ERIC. You kidding me? All's fair in love and war, man. If you got out of Nam by studying philosophy, I wanna shake you hand. You could have been studying the philosophy of the M-16. (*ERIC suddenly leaps to his feet and stands at attention.*) Sir! The M-16 recoiless assault rifle, sir! Clip-loading, gas-operated semiautomatic. Muzzle velocity 3282 feet per second, effective lethal range 440 yards, Sir! (*ERIC sits down on the bench again and resumes a normal conversational tone.*) The shit you remember, man.

PETE. Were you ... I mean ... did you see a lot of action?

ERIC. Did you, Pete?

PETE. What do you mean?

ERIC. You know.

PETE. No, I don't.

ERIC. The beer blasts, man. Them recons in force on the girls' dorms to capture them panties. The home games, man. The action. You couldn't have been studying philosophy all that time, Pete. Tell me about the action.

PETE. I can see you're mocking me. (*PETE stands up.*) Look, Eric, I don't even know how we got into this conversation. I don't know you. You don't know me. I really have to be getting back to my hotel ...

ERIC. Is that where the wife and kids are, Pete? I'd like to meet them. I know I'm dressed a little bit like a bum, man, but I'm not one. Maybe we could all have dinner tonight. A pizza or something, you know? Do the kids like pizza?

PETE. Yes ... but ... well ... they're not here, Eric. They're back in Rochester. I'm in town on business. I fly back tomorrow.

ERIC. What kind of business does a philosopher have in Washington, man?

PETE. I'm not a philosopher. I'm a lobbyist. (*Pause.*) That's someone who tries to persuade legislators and governmental agencies to do certain things which ...

ERIC. I know what a lobbyist is, Pete. I'm not stupid.

PETE. I didn't mean you were stupid.

ERIC. What are you a lobbyist for?

PETE. For the G.P.I.

ERIC. The G.P.I.?

PETE. The Glass Packaging Institute. I try to get legislation favorable to companies that package in glass.

ERIC. Like some other guy who's trying to do the same thing for companies that put things in plastic?

PETE. That's it. "See your way clear to a better America." That's my slogan. Maybe you've heard it?

ERIC. Nope.

PETE. Well, anyway ...

ERIC. And that's what you do?

PETE. Yes.

ERIC. I liked you better when you were a philosopher.

PETE. Well, a man has to do what he can do, doesn't he, Eric? What's your occupation, if I might ask?

ERIC. Temporarily unemployed, Pete.

PETE. Nice work if you can get it

ERIC. No, Pete, it isn't. It really isn't.

PETE. I'm sorry. You having problems?

ERIC. Problems, Pete? Naw! It's just taking me a little while to get my shit together, that's all. It's only been twenty years, man. Any day now, I'm going to find my thing. I'm going to find something nice and solid to get into. Like glass.

PETE. It's easy for you to look down on someone like me, isn't it?

ERIC. Why should I look down on you, man? You got the world by the balls. But I ain't going to be left behind, man. No, I'm not. After all these years, I finally figured out what I was cut out to do.

PETE. What's that?

ERIC. Can I trust you, Pete?

PETE. (*Uncertain.*) Yeah.

(*ERIC unzips his canvas bag and holds it open so PETE can see what's inside.*)

PETE. What's that?

ERIC. C4.

PETE. C4?

ERIC. Plastique.

PETE. Plastique? Plas ... you mean plastic explosive?

ERIC. Not so loud, Pete.

PETE. What in God's name ...? Are you out of your mind?

ERIC. Do I look like I'm out of my mind, Pete?

PETE. It could blow up. You could kill someone.

ERIC. Don't worry, man. It's as harmless as Play Dough until you set it off.

PETE. (*Stands up.*) Listen ... I have to go ...

ERIC. You're gonna try to get a cop, aren't you, man?

PETE. No ...

ERIC. When you come back, I won't be here. And you'll have missed your chance.

PETE. My chance for what?

ERIC. To be a hero. To stop the man who blew up the Vietnam Memorial.

PETE. You're not serious?

ERIC. (*Holds up the canvas bag.*) This says I am.

PETE. But why?

(ERIC reaches into his canvas bag and pulls our a piece of paper. HE unfolds it, and reads.)

ERIC. "To the President of the United States and the Publisher of the Washington Post. I am a Vietnam vet, who served from the years 1968 to 1970. I have nothing but respect in my heart for the men who served in that war, and when I came home, I shared their humiliation. It was not just that our country looked down on us. They didn't even see us. They do not see us today. They have built a memorial for those of us who died. It has become just another Washington tourist attraction, to be seen, photographed and forgotten. No one cares that thousands of Vietnam vets still lead broken lives. No one cares that this year our government spent more on weapons than during any year of the Vietnam War. No one cares that there are now American military advisors in El Salvador. We have learned nothing. The Vietnam Memorial is a sad joke. It is an insult to the memory of the men who served there. To destroy it, as I have done, is an act of love and respect. I am a holder of the Silver Star, which I enclose with this letter. Where I'm going, I won't be needing it. Signed, A vet." *(ERIC slowly folds the paper and puts it back in his bag.)*

PETE. Can I share something with you, Eric?

ERIC. What?

PETE. That is the stupidest letter I've ever heard in my life. It sounds like it was written by a psycho.

ERIC. I'm not a psycho.

PETE. I know that, Eric. But other people aren't going to know that when they read that letter. And what is that bit at the end there? "Where I'm going, I won't be needing it." What is that, Eric? Are you planning to off yourself?

ERIC. Yeah.

PETE. God, Eric, that is such a cliche. And what's this business of signing it: "A vet"? I mean, really, if you're going to do something this big, sign your name to it. Show a little pride.

ERIC. What are you talking like this for, man? You're trying to psych me out or something? That's it, isn't it?

PETE. Not on your life, Eric, my boy. I'm just trying to

straighten you out on a couple of points. Let me tell you what will happen if you succeed with your plan. Everyone — and I mean everyone — will despise you for it. And even with this note, Eric, everyone is going to miss your silly point.

ERIC. It's not a silly point.

PETE. Oh, but it is, Eric. You see, this is not just any war memorial you're looking at here. Americans don't come here so we can feel proud and brave about what we've done. This is a place that reminds us that sometimes men die for nothing. That we are capable of blindness and stupidity and ingratitude. And that makes this the most important war monument ever built. Because it's an anti-war monument. And you're not going to destroy it, Eric. So why don't you just give me the bag?

(PETE reaches out to grab the bag but ERIC clutches it closer. The TWO MEN suddenly become engaged in a silent but violent tug of war. THEY are locked in place, EACH trying to tear the bag out of the other's hand. THEIR EYES are riveted on each other.)

ERIC. *(Spits the words out in a harsh whisper, as HE strains to wrench the bag from Pete's grasp.)* Let go, you fucking college bastard! You weren't there! You don't know! What did you do? What did you fucking ever do?

PETE. I lived, Eric. I survived, goddammit. What did you do?

(With one last pull, ERIC wrenches the bag out of Pete's hands. HE holds it cradled in his arms, like a fallen comrade.)

ERIC. He wouldn't listen, man. I told him, I said, Pete, man, wait'll the reenforcements come in. But he said, come on, and he looked at me with that look he always gave me before we did anything together, and I'd always come along. And that look said he knew I was going to come along, and just then he jumped and started to go and I said, "No, Pete!" and I reached out like this and grabbed his leg, and I guess I slowed him down a little bit, and that's when Charlie opened up from the brush line and caught Pete in the chest. And he might have made it if I hadn't reached out and slowed him down just that little bit. And I knew I'd killed him. And if Pete was dead, I didn't want to be alive. So, I just picked up my weapon and started running toward Charlie, firing. And I was screaming and running straight into the rounds, hoping one of them would take me down. But they didn't. And Pete was dead. And I was alive.

(There is a long pause.)

PETE. The student deferment only lasted a year. Then they had me nailed, Eric. 1A. I was going. Guys I knew were trying anything. If you were a good enough actor, you went down to the draft board and tried to convince them you were queer or crazy, or a conscientious objector. There was this drug I heard about, you took it, and it sent your blood pressure sky-high for about twenty-four hours. They were selling it on campus. Fifty bucks a pop. Everybody was buying it, Eric. It wasn't looked down on. And it was getting guys out. So I bought it. This stuff made you light-headed, and the day I took my physical, I kept feeling like I was going to pass out. And I remember this one bunch of guys, standing around in their jockey shorts, having the time of their lives. Laughing and joking and talking about how they were going to Vietnam to mow down gooks. They were from poor backgrounds. They hadn't been smart enough to go to college and learn to be cowards. When the doctor took my blood pressure, he didn't say anything, but I could see he couldn't believe his eyes. He took it three times. Then he just passed me on to the next station. I figured, it hadn't worked, I was in. The next thing I knew, names were being called, guys were getting right on the bus, and going off to Basic. Then they called my name, and they told me I'd been rejected. And you know what's funny? That's the way I felt. It suddenly felt like I was doing something to be ashamed of. That there was something ... unmanly ... about it. Since that day, I've never talked about it.

(Pause.)

ERIC. We all got our crosses, man. If it makes any difference, I'm glad you told me.

PETE. Eric ...

ERIC. Yeah?

PETE. I haven't known many vets. I mean, it seems like our lives have always gone in different directions. Beginning with that day when they got on the bus and I didn't ...

(Pause.)

ERIC. So what are you trying to say, man?

PETE. I'm just trying to say ... I'm sorry.

(Pause.)

ERIC. You want to know something, Pete? I've been waiting twenty years to hear one of you guys say that.

(ERIC reaches out and grasps Pete's hand. The TWO MEN hold the handshake a long time. Then ERIC stands.)

ERIC. So, Pete ... it's been nice shooting the shit, man. (*HE starts to leave.)*

PETE. Eric, what about the bag

ERIC. What about it, man?

PETE. The explosive.

ERIC. (*Laughs.)* You never been to Nam, Pete. You wouldn't know loaf of plastique from a tuna fish sandwich. And another thing you don't know. Vietnam vets all got fucked-up senses of humor, man. You take care of yourself, now. (*ERIC starts to leave again.)*

PETE. Eric?

ERIC. Yeah?

PETE. You're telling the truth, aren't you?

ERIC. Depends what you call the truth, man. Catch!

(*ERIC tosses the bag at Pete. Instead of catching it, PETE ducks and covers his face with his hands. The bag lands harmlessly in his lap. ERIC laughs.*)

ERIC. It's yours now, man. Where I'm going, I won't be needing it. (*Exits.*)

(*PETE watches ERIC leave, then slowly, gingerly opens the bag. HE takes out the piece of folded paper, unfolds it, and finds it blank on both sides, HE takes out a small square object wrapped in aluminum foil. HE unwraps the foil and discovers a sandwich. HE lays it down on the bench beside him while HE extracts the last article from the bag: a small black case. HE opens it, and slowly removes a medal — the Silver Star. HE holds it out in front of him and watches it twist and catch the light. HE seems mesmerized. Suddenly, HE makes a move to get up, as if he's going to run after Eric. Realizing it's too late, HE continues to look at the medal. HE holds it up to his own chest. His whole body slowly braces itself into a position of military attention. HE freezes as the LIGHTS slowly fade to BLACK.*)

END OF PLAY

COSTUME PLOT

PETE:
Blue suit
Blue shirt
Red tie
Black shoes

ERIC:
Blue jeans
Plaid flannel shirt
Army fatigue jacket
Sneakers

PROPERTY PLOT

Park bench
Canvas carrying bag – Eric
> In:
>> Foil-wrapped tuna fish sandwich
>> Foil-wrapped hero sandwich
>> Blank sheet of white paper
>> Black leather case
>> A Silver Star

Small color snapshot of a woman – Eric
35 millimeter Nikon SLR camera – Pete
Wallet (breast pocket type) – Pete
> In:
>> Color snapshots of young boy and young girl

SET DESIGN

Very minimal. A park bench, center stage. A ligh wash may be
employed to create the effect of dappled sunlight.

Larry Cadman

Larry Cadman lives and works in New York City.

SOMETHING ROTTEN IN DENMARK

by Annie G.

Something Rotten In Denmark was produced at the Harold Clurman Theater as part of the Playwrights Horizons Theatre Festival, in New York City, in August, 1991. It was directed by Mike Wills. The cast was as follows:

CORNELIA ....Maggie Wysocki[*]
MARY..Denise Krueger[*]
ANN...Marta Vidal
JASON...Ben Shepard[*]
BARTHOLEMEW ....Marc Parent
GHOST ....Patrick Johnson

Something Rotten In Denmark was produced at the Nat Horne Theatre, in New York City, in June 1993. It was directed by Mike Wills. The cast was as follows:

CORNELIUS ....Tony Lombardi[*]
MARY ....Maggie Wysocki[*]
ANN ....Annie G.[*]
JASON...Ben Shepard[*]
BARTHOLEMEW...Jeff Hoyer
GHOST...Paul Lima[*]

[*] These cast members also performed at the Edinburgh Festival Fringe, August 1992.

CHARACTERS

CORNELIUS — apprentice to Mary
ANNIE H. — wife of the playwright
MARY — costume mistress
JASON — an actor, director
BARTHOLEMEW — an actor, director
GHOST — a ghost

TIME & PLACE

16th Century England.

A costume room.

This play is dedicated to my mommy
who art in heaven.

SOMETHING ROTTEN IN DENMARK

LIGHTS up on a costume room in 16th century England.

CORNELIUS. Oh what a beautiful morning! First day of rehearsal, and little me, little insignificant me, a small but important cog in the wheel, apprentice at Bill's great theatre. I'll do the sweeping, I'll do the dirty work, I'll play the parts nobody wants to play, I'll climb every mountain, right to the top and then I'll be the best actor this theatre has ever seen. I can do it, I know I can, I'll be swell, I'll be great, gonna have the whole world on a plate. If I have to be a ditch digger for the rest of my life, I'll be a ditch digger who once had a wonderful day, it only takes a moment. I had a dream, a dream about me baby, it's gonna come true baby. I know, I'm just a cockeyed optimist, but I look out the window and I see the hills are alive. You have to start at the bottom, and I do love sweeping. It makes me dream the impossible dream and want to dance all night. So many things to look forward to, and so many things to learn and so many things to plan. The shipment! I almost forgot about the shipment, I must rush off and attend to it. What a day! Makes me think everything's coming up roses!

(Exit CORNELIUS, enter ANNE.)

ANNE. Mary!

(Enter MARY.)

MARY. Anne!
ANNE. Have you seen my husband?
MARY. No, I haven't seen Bill all day.

ANNE. I'm disturbed, distressed and distracted.

MARY. Do tell.

ANNE. This plume came from my garden. It's not from a bird, at least not from a little creature that flies, but from a creature of another sort, I'm wondering do you recognize it?

MARY. A lot of plumes are in and out of here.

ANNE. Thought you'd have some ideas, though, on whose it was. Oh well, I've got a notion, but I must be sure who it belongs to. I'm off to rehearsal.

(ANNE exits, enter JASON.)

JASON. I'm sick and tired of getting these rotten, stinking, no good parts. There's absolutely no reason for my character to be in the play.

MARY. It's the lead character.

JASON. It's a poorly written lead character.

MARY. Did you come for a fitting?

JASON. No, I'm in the middle of rehearsal and I'm not going back.

MARY. Ever?

JASON. No, not ever, never, I mean not never. He's supposed to be a prince. What kind of prince is that? When Willie said he wrote a part for me I thought it would be something big, juicy and meaty. Not some wimp who can't make up his mind.

MARY. Oh, poor Jason.

JASON. You're the only one who understands me.

MARY. It's not that difficult.

(Enter BARTHOLEMEW.)

BARTHOLEMEW. Jason, are you coming back to rehearsal?

JASON. Why should I? This play stinks! He promised me a great role, and what does he give me? A wuss. A wuss with a stupid name! He might as well have called it Pig-Meat. Willie doesn't know a thing about writing.

BARTHOLEMEW. Jason, give it a chance.

JASON. What do you mean give it a chance? It doesn't make any sense, why would he want to kill his uncle? There's nothing in the text to substantiate it. He's completely happy, he's a prince, he lives in a castle, he has lots of friends. He's got everything going for him. And the transitions are horrible. One minute he's happy to see his love and the next he's sending her to a nunnery! And why doesn't he start talking until page five?

BARTHOLEMEW. Jason, get off your high chair and look at what's in front of you.

JASON. It's not exactly Sophocles, you know.

BARTHOLEMEW. It's a wonderful play, it's the best thing Bill's ever written.

JASON. Oh please. Look at the way the characters speak in this play. No one talks this way. Verse, rhymes! Puh! Say by some remote possibility, Willie's plays do survive, will people five hundred years from now, think this is how we talked! Besides, I've heard tell that he doesn't even write his own plays!

BARTHOLEMEW. Look, I've got to finish this rehearsal. Are you coming back in?

JASON. No.

BARTHOLEMEW. Jason, this play goes up in three weeks, what would you like me to do?

JASON. You play the bloody role! And I'll direct.

BARTHOLEMEW. Jason, you don't really mean that.

JASON. Don't I? You should play the bad role, you always get the good roles. It's not fair!

BARTHOLEMEW. Do you really want me to play the prince? Would that you make happy?

JASON. Happier.

MARY. So, Bartholemew's to play the lead?

BARTHOLEMEW. Yes.

MARY. Very well then, you're so much larger than Jason. That means another costume.

JASON. I'm the director now, let's finish rehearsing this toad.

MARY. May I have a moment more with Bartholemew, please. I must get his measurements.

JASON. You have five minutes. (*Exits.*)

BARTHOLEMEW. That fool! He wouldn't know a good role if it came and smacked him in the face. Little upstart! He was a peon, the ticket taker, turn my back for a second and he's getting all of the good roles, I used to get! I'm getting older daily and he seems to be getting younger by the minute. He's making my life miserable. Mary, I need a sword. I want to play this part with a sword.

MARY. Yes, we have the sword for you, but I'm sure yours will do quite nicely.

BARTHOLEMEW. I need a sheath, I want to place my sword in a sheath.

MARY. I've just the sheath for your sword.

BARTHOLEMEW. Yes Mary, I know your sheath. I want to bury my sword deep within your sheath.

MARY. Way up high.

BARTHOLEMEW. Higher.

MARY. Higher.

BARTHOLEMEW. Oh Mary, what is it you do to me? Right after rehearsal we'll have another fitting. Of the sword I mean.

(Exit BARTHOLEMEW, enter CORNELIUS.)

CORNELIUS. I've the tambourines ordered for the play. Don't ya just love 'em? Makes me think of the time when I ... *(Sings.)* Saw a rabbit with a cat, they scat by in seconds flat ...

MARY. Not now Cornelius!

(Exit CORNELIUS, enter ANNE.)

ANNE. Where is everyone?

(JASON and BARTHOLEMEW run across stage behind Annie.)

ANNE. They're not at rehearsal, where can they be?

(JASON and BARTHOLEMEW run back across stage.)

ANNE. What's going on?

MARY. Oh, have some faith. They'll pull together in the end.

ANNE. Faith? Their pulling together is exactly what I'm concerned about. A lot of things get created by people pushing and pulling together. And now all evidence in front of my face can not be ignored. Purple plumes, I ask you.

MARY. What exactly are you asking me?

ANNE. They're avoiding me, they must be.

MARY. Me thinkst you wax desperate with imagination.

ANNE. Things are not as they were and not as they seem. There's something rotten in the state of Britain. That's good, I must write that down. Help me find the owner of this purple plume, it's of dire interest to me. Who, who, who?

(Enter JASON.)

JASON. Stop what you're doing.

ANNE. Jason.

JASON. Anne!

ANNE. Where is everyone? What is going on with this rehearsal?

JASON. We, uh, kind of came to a stop, a little problem. Nothing important, Willie had to go do a rewrite.

ANNE. What do you mean rewrite? Why would he go do a thing like that? Where could he be? I must find him. (*Exits.*)

JASON. Mary, listen here, don't tell Anne about the switch that Bartholemew and I made. She was rather helpful in helping me land this role. She won't like it if she finds out I'm not doing it.

MARY. Oh, don't worry your little head. Mum's the word.

JASON. Now, where's Bartholemew?

MARY. I sent him off to you.

JASON. Excellent. I have a concept, I've decided the prince is a woman. It only makes sense. No man would be so indecisive. Forget the princely togs, design a dress.

MARY. A dress?! Bartholemew would look stupid in a dress.

JASON. Yes!

MARY. Well then, if a dress is what you want, then a dress is what you'll get.

JASON. And furthermore, whatever Bartholemew says, don't give him the sword.

MARY. Why would I give him the sword, now that he's to play a woman?

JASON. It's our sword for our little passion plays.

(Exit JASON, enter CORNELIUS.)

CORNELIUS. Mary, I've the tambourines and streamers ordered for the play. Oh I do fancy these streamers in all the lovely colors. *(Sings.)* I gotta cow who jumps through hoops, sings a song and eats Fruit Loops ...

MARY. Not now Cornelius!

(Exit CORNELIUS, enter ANNE.)

ANNE. Where are all those men?

(JASON and BARTHOLEMEW run across the stage behind Anne.)

ANNE. I'm losing my patience, I'm tired of trying to track them down.

(JASON and BARTHOLEMEW run back across the stage.)

ANNE. What am I to do?

MARY. You can stay right here and help me with some sewing.

ANNE. I can't do that. I've a mission I must accomplish. I've a quest. I'm questing. One can't stay ignorant, even though it is bliss. Can't stay in the dark, light the candle. Who are you, who are you I say? Get out of the flower bed and stand in the light. Caught your radish in the garden. All it takes is one seed, one feather. If the other eye offends thee pluck it out. Plucking little chickadees! What is Bill thinking? What will he think? I think, you think, we think, they all think! A woman knows. She knows I say!

MARY. Anne, darling you're a little excited. Take a couple of deep breaths.

ANNE. I don't have time for breathing. I'm very busy. I must find out who's the owner of this plume.

MARY. You must screw your courage to the sticking place.

ANNE. Screw your courage, that's good. I must write that down. Can use it for the next play. I'm off to the stage.

(ANNE exits, enter BARTHOLEMEW.)

BARTHOLEMEW. VICTORY, VICTORY, VICTORY! Ah, ha, ha, ha, ha, ha, ha that little fool! Whatever Jason hands out, I'm up for it. Foil, ho! Pounce, ho! My chance at reclaiming my title as *the* actor of the company is here. Jason has the stupidest ideas, but I play them as if they're brilliant!

MARY. But you are brilliant, and ever so charming.

BARTHOLEMEW. As are you my little lotus petal. Ha, ha, pounce, swish, I'm up for it, I'm up for it!

MARY. As you always are.

BARTHOLEMEW. I'm going to pound his trifling ego to the wall, and come out the victor.

MARY. Pounding and swishing, yum!

BARTHOLEMEW. I'm a prince! I'm a woman! I'm a snake! Whatever he hands out!

MARY. Oh, I would so like to see you as a snake.

BARTHOLEMEW. Slithering to your heart.

MARY. With passion a glare.

BARTHOLEMEW. I'm everything, everything he wants and more. More! O, what a rogue and peasant slave am I! Is it not monstrous that this player here, But in a fiction, in a dream of passion, Could force his soul so to his own conceit, that, from her working, all his visage waned, Tears in his eyes, distraction in's aspect, A broken voice, and his whole function suiting, With forms to his conceit? And all for nothing!

MARY. It's never for nothing.

BARTHOLEMEW. My darling pet, you're my inspiration, I dedicate my performance to you. For Hecuba! Must get back to rehearsal.

MARY. Oh, you leave me breathless.

(Exit BARTHOLEMEW, enter CORNELIUS.)

CORNELIUS. Mary, I've the tambourines, streamers and balloons. They do strange things to me ... *(Sings.)* Gonna make a pumpkin pie, bake it right up to the sky ...

MARY. Not now Cornelius!

(Exit CORNELIUS, enter JASON.)

JASON. *(Entering.)* Damn that man! Damn Bartholemew! He's much too good as a woman. I can't have that! He's back to playing a man!

MARY. A man?!

JASON. Yes! And furthermore, I've a concept. This whole play is based on the fact that he's a prince and tied to the throne, therefore we must show this symbolically. We'll have a red cord coming from the navel, as in the umbilical cord, and we will attach it to a throne. Build it in the costume, so it follows him everywhere. Everywhere the Prince may go, the throne is not far behind.

MARY. You're joking?

JASON. No I'm not. And furthermore, I've been successful at keeping Anne at bay.

MARY. Your goings are going to be rather costly for you.

JASON. Too steep to mention. If you see her, keep her from the stage, send her to the river. Tell her Willie's doing a rewrite there and desperately wants to see her.

MARY. Why do I submit to your whims?

JASON. Because you're an angel. Make sure the costume you create is really, really stupid. And make it foul. Fair is foul and foul is fair

(Exit JASON, enter ANNE.)

MARY. To sew or not to sew that is the question. Whether 'tis nobler in the mind to suffer the slings and arrows of outrageous actors or to take up arms with a clothful of needles ...

ANNE. Oh, that's good, I must write that down. We can put it somewhere in the play. I'll tell Bill, as soon as I can find him. Where are all those men?!

(JASON and BARTHOLEMEW crisscross behind Annie and collide.)

ANNE. I think they still exist.

(JASON and BARTHOLEMEW notice Annie and sneak quietly off.)

ANNE. You're very good.

MARY. So people keep telling me.

ANNE. Let not the bloat King tempt you to bed.

MARY. Well I was hoping quite the opposite.

ANNE. Mary, we must be careful. They put seeds in your belly then disappear, and you're left with a melon the size of the Armada and a feather. Put a feather in your cap and call it macaroni.

MARY. Anne, I'm beginning to be a little concerned about you.

ANNE. Concerns? You have concerns? I've become a garden for fruits and vegetables. Squash, radish, berries, bellies! Plucked a feather from a tree. Who so owns this feather and why was it in my bed? Who's in my bed? Why's in my bed? Wherefore art thou Romeo? Deny thy father, who is thy father? Does he exist I'm not sure! I've been consumed by the fruits and vegetables of thy labor! My belly's full. Tomatoes, potatoes, sprouts, broccoli, cauliflower, rhubarb, rutabaga, raspberry, strawberry, gooseberry, dewberry, beriberi ...

MARY. I think I heard Bill was down by the river waiting for you.

ANNE. Bill? River? I'm off! Blackberry, blueberry, boysenberry, huckleberry, elderberry, bearbelly ...

(Exit ANNE, enter CORNELIUS.)

CORNELIUS. ... tambourines, streamers, balloons, ribbons, horns, flowers, candy ...

MARY. Stop! Don't even think about it!

(Exit CORNELIUS, enter JASON.)

JASON. Damn that man! Damn Bartholemew! He's much too good as a man! I can't have that. All my work will be for nought. He's ruining my life. There's only one solution. I must kill him. Now where's that sword?

MARY. You're joking?

JASON. Where's that sword?

MARY. It's lost.

JASON. It's not lost, you've put it away.

MARY. Well, I've forgotten where I put it.

JASON. Well, unforget where you put it.

MARY. I can't unforget where I put it.

JASON. I bet it's back in the wardrobe.

(Exit JASON, enter BARTHOLEMEW.)

BARTHOLEMEW. My little pigeon.

MARY. You must go.

BARTHOLEMEW. You have another lover?

MARY. No, it's your life. Run!

BARTHOLEMEW. Nonsense, you're protecting your lover.

MARY. You're my only lover.

BARTHOLEMEW. I loved you not.

MARY. I was the more deceived.

BARTHOLEMEW. Liar!!! Who is your lover?!!!

MARY. I thought he was you, you made me believe so.

BARTHOLEMEW. Dishonest woman! Get thee to a nunnery!

MARY. You're confusing your life with the script!

BARTHOLEMEW. I'll find him myself. Say back in the wardrobe.

(Exit BARTHOLEMEW, enter JASON.)

JASON. I can't find it. You must unforget, you must unforget!

MARY. I left it by the river.

JASON. Nonsense, that's the lie I told you to tell Anne. I bet I didn't look hard enough. I bet it is in the wardrobe.

(Exit JASON, enter BARTHOLEMEW.)

BARTHOLEMEW. You must have given him some signal. Where is he? Who is he?

MARY. Speak to me no more!

BARTHOLEMEW. Rank sweat of an enseamed bed, honeying and making love over the nasty sty!

MARY. You're the only nasty sty around here!

BARTHOLEMEW. Who is he?

(Enter JASON with sword in hand.)

JASON. Ho! Ho! How now? A rat? Dead for a ducat, dead!

BARTHOLEMEW. Jason!

JASON. Bart! Unhand her! I'm here to take your life Bartholemew, give it up.

BARTHOLEMEW. No!

JASON. But you have to! I have the sword. Either you give it up or I take it!

BARTHOLEMEW. What is he doing with our sword?

JASON. What do you mean our sword? Did you play bury the sword with him?

BARTHOLEMEW. Yes.

MARY. But it's over now, because you're going to die. Kill him, Jason.

BARTHOLEMEW. Mary!

MARY. You sacrificed my heart, now go ahead, die!

JASON. Here I go, I'm going to kill you now!

MARY. Do it!

JASON. I'm trying!

(A musical CHORD is heard. Enter GHOST, visible only to JASON.)

GHOST. Not good enough!

(A second CHORD is heard.)

GHOST. I shall be avenged!!!!!!
JASON. Angels of grace defend us! Who are you?
GHOST. I am the ghost of the poorly performed parts!

(A CHORD is heard.)

JASON. Oh, my prophetic soul!
BARTHOLEMEW. Who are you talking to?
JASON. Do you see or hear nothing?
BARTHOLEMEW. No!
JASON. Be thou a spirit of heaven or a goblin damn'd.
GHOST. You created me! There are more things in heaven and hell than are dreamt of in your philosophy.
MARY. Who are you talking to?
BARTHOLEMEW. Why do you want to kill me anyway?
JASON. You're too damn good an actor! I hate you!
GHOST. My hour is almost come, when I to sulph'rous and tormenting flames must render up myself.
JASON. Alas, poor ghost!
GHOST. I shall be avenged!

(A CHORD is heard. EVERYONE is magically thrown about.)

BARTHOLEMEW. Jason, what strange and supernatural powers you have today!
MARY. Alas, he's mad!
JASON and GHOST. Good and mad!
BARTHOLEMEW. What do you mean too damn good? This is nonsense!
JASON. You're ruining my life!

BARTHOLEMEW. I don't mean to, I'm just doing the best I can.

(A CHORD is heard and BARTHOLEMEW is pinned on his back.)

GHOST. Revenge this foul and fearsome talent!
BARTHOLEMEW. I can't move!
MARY. Wormwood! Wormwood!
GHOST. Kill said beastly actor!
MARY. Kill said bloody vermin!
GHOST Kill him!
MARY. Kill him!
GHOST and MARY. Kill!
JASON. Here I go!
BARTHOLEMEW. Wait!
JASON. Why should I?
BARTHOLEMEW. We can work something out. I think you're a pretty damn good actor, too, sometimes.
JASON. Honest?
BARTHOLEMEW. I heard thee speak me a speech once, it pleas'd not the million, 'twas cavalry to the general, but it was well spoken, with good accent and good discretion.
JASON. Did you really think so?
BARTHOLEMEW. No.

(A CHORD is heard and BARTHOLEMEW rolls across stage. A second CHORD is heard and BARTHOLEMEW rolls back.)

BARTHOLEMEW. Yes, your powers and strength are impressing me more and more each moment.
JASON. You don't mean it.
BARTHOLEMEW. Don't I? I've got a solution. Would it please you if I stepped down, and you played the Prince?
GHOST. Don't accept the first offer, see what more you can get.
JASON. I don't know.
BARTHOLEMEW We'll have Mary create you a fabulous

costume.

MARY. I will not!

GHOST. Ah yes, fair seamstress, sew.

MARY. Inspiration. Must sew.

GHOST. Furthermore, the play's too long.

JASON. It must be shorter.

BARTHOLEMEW. I'll have Bill do a rewrite.

GHOST. What else?

JASON. What else?

BARTHOLEMEW. You'll have roses thrown at your feet, top billing.

JASON. Well?

BARTHOLEMEW. I'll work with you closely, you'll be hailed as a fabulous actor, as a fabulous prince, and I don't use that word lightly. I'll help you in every which way I can, whatever may be required of me.

GHOST. Make him swear by the sword.

(A CHORD is heard. BARTHOLEMEW is forced to his knees.)

JASON. Swear by the sword.

BARTHOLEMEW. I swear.

GHOST. Take it.

JASON. I'll take it.

BARTHOLEMEW. Alright then, get that sword out of my face. Settled. It's really rather a good part, you'll see.

GHOST. I'll be watching, and remember, if this remains another poorly performed part, I shall return. I shall be avenged!!!!!!

(A CHORD is heard, exit the GHOST. HE spins JASON and BARTHOLEMEW as he goes.)

MARY. You're not going to kill him?

JASON. Well, we've reached an understanding.

MARY. Oh great, give me back that sword.

JASON. It's mine.

BARTHOLEMEW. No it's not, it's mine.

JASON. You can't have it. Get away.

BARTHOLEMEW. Give it here.

MARY. No, it's my sword. Neither of you can ever have it.

JASON. No, it's mine, it's mine. I want to play bury the sword in Mary.

(During the struggle, JASON plunges the sword into Mary. MARY slowly pulls the sword from her body.)

JASON and BARTHOLEMEW. BLOOD!!

(MARY staggers and falls.)

BARTHOLEMEW. Look what you've done.

MARY. Not dead yet.

BARTHOLEMEW. Oh, sorry.

MARY. Either this wallpaper goes, or I do. (*Dies.*)

BARTHOLEMEW. You've killed her. You fool.

JASON. I just know this will ruin my acting career.

BARTHOLEMEW. Is that all you can think of?

JASON. Well we can't bring her back, can we? We have to hide her. We'll give her a proper burial at the stroke of midnight. You must help me.

BARTHOLEMEW. No!

JASON. You have to. This won't look good for you either. And besides you swore by the sword to help in any way required.

BARTHOLEMEW. So I did.

JASON. We have to hide her fast.

JASON and BARTHOLEMEW. Where, where, where? The wardrobe!

(THEY start to hide the body. Enter CORNELIUS.)

CORNELIUS. Oh Mary ...

JASON and BARTHOLEMEW. Not now, Cornelius!

(Exit CORNELIUS, enter ANNE.)

ANNE. So here you all are, I will not be ignored.

JASON. Anne!

ANNE. I've looked and looked, and no people, no bodies, only trees, orchards, peach trees, river. Where, where, where have you been?

JASON. We've been working out the wardrobe.

BARTHOLEMEW. Costumes!

JASON. Costumes! Yes!

BARTHOLEMEW. Yes!

JASON. Yes!

BARTHOLEMEW. Yes!

JASON. We've been having a little trouble. Nothing outrageous.

BARTHOLEMEW. No!

JASON. No!

BARTHOLEMEW. No!

JASON. No!

ANNE. Outrageous? You've been hiding from me.

JASON. Hide?

BARTHOLEMEW. Hide?

JASON. I don't know what you're talking about ...

JASON and BARTHOLEMEW. ... We've nothing to hide!

ANNE. You can't deny it, I know, I know all.

JASON. What do you know?

ANNE. I'm pregnant with your child.

JASON. No you're not!

ANNE. Then I'm pregnant with your child.

BARTHOLEMEW What!

ANNE. Oh don't you just not care. Fill the vessel, water the plants and run when the flowers begin to grow.

BARTHOLEMEW. Where's Bill? Does he know of you like this?

ANNE. He's nowhere to be found. Does he exist, I'm not sure? Is anyone of us what we say we are? They say the owl was the baker's daughter. Lord, we know what we are, but know not what we may be. A plume, a purple plume. I demand an answer.

JASON. What's the question?

ANNE. Whose cap doth it belongth to?

BARTHOLEMEW. Jason did you not wear a hat with such a plume, when first you played the young lead? Yes, it belongs to Jason. I remember the first time you wore that hat, oh you did prance about in it. Proud as a peacock, did you not. "Oh look everyone my hat. That means I have the lead, that means Bartholemew does not have the lead." I remember quite well.

JASON. So, what if I did, what does it mean?

ANNE. Did you wear said hat, on a balmy day, fertile night, ground moist, beckoning? Oh come to me, we can see if we can fly. Meet you in the garden, behind the rhododendrons, come hither my pet.

BARTHOLEMEW. Oh, Jason this is jolly good. Yet another ace up my sleeve.

JASON. Shut up, Bart! When exactly did this happen?

ANNE. Six weeks to the day, tick tock, tick tock.

JASON. Six weeks? That was the time of the May Day Costume Ball. When you, Bartholemew, said you had to borrow my hat, to fit a particular costume, to please a certain lover! Ah, yes, I remember it quite well!

ANNE. Exactly May Day, feathery night. I plucked a feather from my lover's hat, laid it on the flower bed, the father of my peach tree, I kept it on the flower bed till I was sure. And now I'm sure as I can be.

JASON. Oh isn't this just too delicious?

BARTHOLEMEW. How can you be so certain?

ANNE. A woman knows, a woman knows.

JASON. So now I've got the lead, and you're in a compromising position.

BARTHOLEMEW. You're so obvious.

JASON. You want the same things as I, only this time round, you lost.

ANNE. Now I'm certain, I've got what I come for. I know whose nose my sprout will spring.

BARTHOLEMEW. Nose? What about my nose?

ANNE. Heredity! Can't be too careful. Not any seed will do for my sprout. Must be concerned with nose, good teeth, tall stature, strong thigh and yummy cucumber. Ah yes, will do, will do.

BARTHOLEMEW. Look, Anne, be reasonable. Don't go do anything rash. We don't want to upset Bill.

ANNE. Wouldn't think of it. Don't fret, he'll never know our little secret. He'll believe the babe is from his own seed. O, how the wheel becomes it! Must go share the good news. Daddy, Daddy if you could only see, just how good he's been treating me ... (*Sings.*) but I made up my mind, I'm keeping my baby. Ohh, I'm gonna keep my baby ... (*Exits.*)

JASON. Well, well, well, look what's just been unearthed.

BARTHOLEMEW. You heard her, she won't implicate me in anything scandalous to Bill.

JASON. Yes, but some certain actor might whisper in his ear.

BARTHOLEMEW. I wouldn't be so eager to go prattling about. I may have caused a life to commence, but you killed a woman.

JASON. It's not just any womb you invaded.

BARTHOLEMEW. The crime for which I have been accused does not carry the death sentence.

JASON. It would be death to your career as an actor if Willie were to find out about the May Day impregnation.

BARTHOLEMEW. If one word is so much as spoken by you, I will march off to the authorities.

JASON. Don't threaten me, I can conjure up supernatural powers just like that.

(*A CHORD is heard. Enter MARY and the GHOST.*)

GHOST. So glad to meet you. You'll like being a ghost, you get to choose who can see and hear you. And shake up those who refuse to learn their lessons.

(*With a magical gesture a CHORD is heard. JASON is thrown to the floor.*)

MARY. Fantastic! You mean I can throttle the vermin who dumped me for naught?!

(MARY makes the same gesture and a CHORD is heard. BARTHOLEMEW is thrown to the floor.)

MARY. I'm an eager student of your abilities.
GHOST. Our lessons shall commence. I keep my goods in a little alcove.
MARY. Goods? What might those be?
GHOST. Whips, chains, slime.
MARY. Oh, and used for what? Pray tell.
GHOST. Let's see if you can discover.
MARY. You're fascinating. I bet you were an actor.
GHOST. Yes, and let me tell you, I played a slew of poorly performed parts.
MARY. I have yet to meet an actor dead or alive who hasn't.
GHOST. To the alcove!

(A CHORD is heard. MARY makes a gesture, and BARTHOLEMEW and JASON bang their heads on the floor. Exit the GHOST and MARY.)

JASON. Damn that ghost! I could kill him!
BARTHOLEMEW. Damn that woman! I could kill her!
JASON. Look here Bartie, you are going to help me, aren't you?
BARTHOLEMEW. Don't start calling me Bartie.
JASON. Seems to me we're at an impasse. Stalemate.
BARTHOLEMEW. What of it?
JASON. We're both in compromising positions, the only thing to do is to work together.
BARTHOLEMEW. Yes, you're right. Well then, let's begin. If you want to be a great actor, you have to concentrate and focus, and not let anything in your life ever affect your work. If you listen to me, I'll make you the finest Prince of Denmark ever. Speak the first speech, I pray you, trippingly on the tongue. But if you mouth

it, as many of our players do, I had as lief the town crier spoke my lines.

JASON. Nor do not saw the air too much with your hand, thus, but use all gently.

BARTHOLEMEW. For in the very torrent, tempest, and, as I may say, whirlwind of your passion ...

JASON. You must acquire and beget a temperance that may give it smoothness.

BARTHOLEMEW. All the world's a stage.

JASON. It's about life!

BARTHOLEMEW. Madness!

JASON. Blood!

BARTHOLEMEW Guts!

JASON. Wine!

BARTHOLEMEW. Women!

JASON. Song!

JASON and BARTHOLEMEW. It's, it's, it's about ... COTTON! Now, Cornelius, now!

(CORNELIUS comes running out with tambourine singing to the tune of "Pick a Bale of Cotton," the old Afro-American folk song, using these lyrics)

CORNELIUS.
Gotta jump down turn around pick a bale of cotton
Gotta jump down turn around pick a bale a day

(The entire ENSEMBLE comes out and joins CORNELIUS in song and dance.)

Gotta jump down turn around pick a bale of cotton
Gotta jump down turn around pick a bale a day

Gonna make a pumpkin pie
Bake it right up to the sky

Gotta jump down turn around pluck a patch of turnips

Gotta jump down turn around pluck a patch a day
Gotta jump down turn around pluck a patch of turnips
Gotta jump down turn around pluck a patch a day

Saw a rabbit with a cat
They scat by in seconds flat

Gotta jump down turn around shake a leg in May
Gotta jump down turn around shake a leg a day
Gotta jump down turn around shake a leg in May
Gotta jump down turn around shake a leg a day

I gotta cow who jumps through hoops
Sings a song and eat Fruit Loops

Gotta jump down turn around fricassee a chicken
Gotta jump down turn around fricassee a day
Gotta jump down turn around fricassee a chicken
Gotta jump down turn around fricassee a day

I don't know but I've been told
What you know ain't always so

It ain't?

(EVERYONE starts tossing candy to the audience and balloons fall.)

Gotta jump down turn around pick a bale of cotton
Gotta jump down turn around pick a bale a day
Gotta jump down turn around pick a bale of cotton
Gotta jump down turn around pick a bale a day
Oh Lordy, pick a bale of cotton
Oh Lordy, pick a bale a day

(Song ends. The CAST collapses.)

BLACKOUT!

THE END

Annie G.

Annie G. wrote *G-Force* seen at the Edinburgh Festival (nominated for Best of the Fringe), *Experiment at the Asylum* (which had a long run Off-Broadway, as well as being seen in Budapest, Hungary), *13 Steps of Judgment Day, Open and Shut* and *G-Man. In-Communicado* had a main stage reading at Playwrights Horizons. She wrote for *Where's the Party* seen on ABC-TV.

HOW MANY TO TANGO?

by

Sandra J. Albert

How Many To Tango? was produced at The Common Basis Theatre April 23rd-May 10th 1993. It was directed by Marcia Haufrecht with the following cast:

ELEANOR...Janis Blair

BOBBY ....Charlie Kelley

How Many To Tango? was subsequently presented in the Eighteenth Annual Off-Off Broadway Short Play Festival.

For Dorothy

HOW MANY TO TANGO?

Scene 1

A table and two chairs in a SPOTLIGHT.

AT RISE: ELEANOR, an attractive woman in her early thirties, sits alone at the table trying to be composed as SHE sips a coffee. SHE is dressed all in black: tights, sweater, and mini skirt.

SHE glances at her watch and looks around, her eyes searching beyond the circle of light. Seeing nothing, SHE opens her handbag, finds a stray piece of paper, and starts reading it. Anything to stop fidgeting.

Finally, BOBBY, a tall, very handsome man in trim, athletic shape, in his mid-thirties, enters.

HE wears jeans, a shirt and a jacket. HE walks directly up to her.

BOBBY. Hi. I got a little behind.

ELEANOR. I was giving you another ten minutes, then I was leaving.

BOBBY. (*Genuinely embarrassed.*) I'm sorry. I'm usually not late, but you couldn't know that. Did you think I was standing you up? (*Sits down across from her.*)

ELEANOR. I was going to think about that in ten minutes.

BOBBY. I'm glad you waited. I'm really sorry. (*Staring at her.*) You look different. Your face is thinner.

ELEANOR. You look different, too.

BOBBY. What's different about me?

ELEANOR. You're taller.

BOBBY. I was sitting down, wasn't I?

ELEANOR. I guess my depth perception isn't that good.

BOBBY. Why do you have to say things like that?

ELEANOR. I don't know. I need a drink.

BOBBY. This is a coffee shop.

ELEANOR. That's the problem. I know I picked the place but I

63

didn't think I'd feel this way. You want a coffee?

BOBBY. No. I don't drink coffee. What way?

ELEANOR. Nervous. I'll just finish this. Then we can go for a drink. If you don't mind.

BOBBY. Let's talk for a minute.

ELEANOR. Okay. I feel a little better. It was just that first minute seeing you. So tall.

BOBBY. All those late night telephone calls. I feel like I already know everything about you.

ELEANOR. I did all the talking. I guess I get vulnerable at two A.M. So you think there's nothing left to know about?

BOBBY. I feel close to you.

ELEANOR. Oh. Well. I don't think I know you at all. Your hair is so perfect.

BOBBY. I like your hair.

ELEANOR. You do? The color you mean?

BOBBY. Everything.

ELEANOR. Thank you. But your hair, you know, it's absolutely perfect. I can't imagine what it must be like to be you.

BOBBY. What's it like? Everyone thinks you're stupid and that you get everything. That you don't have to work for anything. Growing up, people took one look at me and hated me. I didn't shave for seven years — most of my twenties. I grew it all over and even under my neck.

ELEANOR. Did that help?

BOBBY. It let me feel invisible. I worked as a waiter and studied acting until I finally had the nerve to shave it off. It's been five years.

ELEANOR. So what's it like now?

BOBBY. I'm trying to deal with it. I'm in therapy.

ELEANOR. I bet you brush women off like gnats. When you were eating your hamburger all alone at a table I noticed you, but I could never have talked to you. It was because Marilyn was your neighbor and introduced us, otherwise, I'd never meet anyone like you.

BOBBY. Why like gnats?

ELEANOR. It's a fly that attacks humans and sucks their

blood.

BOBBY. I was with one woman for twelve years and she left me for another man while I was supporting her. I guess she was a gnat.

ELEANOR. Twelve years. Why didn't you marry her?

BOBBY. She was a woman like your mother.

ELEANOR. My mother?

BOBBY. You said she spent most of her time thinking about herself.

ELEANOR. Well shopping. She couldn't help it. When she was all dressed up, she looked beautiful. I think my mother could have been a movie star. And even though she wasn't, she was, sort of. She even wore those cat glasses with rhinestones on them. She had a lot of long white gloves. (SHE makes a gesture as if trying one of them on.) I have them now.

BOBBY. I'm sorry.

ELEANOR. It's all right. I told you it's been almost a year since she died. I'll never wear the gloves but I like looking at them.

BOBBY. It doesn't make up for the way she was. Ignoring who you were.

ELEANOR. Is this a therapy session or a date?

BOBBY. You told me about her.

ELEANOR. Why did you stay?

BOBBY. What?

ELEANOR. Why did you stay with her?

BOBBY. I used to think things were forever.

ELEANOR. I used to think that, too.

BOBBY. I went into therapy for her. If she could only have waited. I would have married her when I was ready. She was supposed to wait.

ELEANOR. How long ago?

BOBBY. How long ago what?

ELEANOR. Did it end? Your relationship.

BOBBY. Two years. I'm not interested in that kind of relationship again. Believe me.

ELEANOR. It's terrible when you lose someone you love.

BOBBY. Yeah.

ELEANOR. I like talking to you.

BOBBY. I like talking to you, too.

ELEANOR. Can I tell you something?

BOBBY. Sure.

ELEANOR. Well, one thing I always wanted was to be dipped. You know how I mean?

BOBBY. Dipped?

ELEANOR. Yes. See. That's something you didn't know about me. Like in the tango when you're kind of bent backwards with one foot in the air.

BOBBY. Oh yes. I know. Why did you tell me that?

ELEANOR. Because I wanted you to know that I'm not only somebody who works in the contracts department of a publishing house. I'm not in show business but I have dreams, too.

BOBBY. (*Looking at his watch.*) Look, I have to go.

ELEANOR. You do? So soon?

BOBBY. I have to meet my scene partner. It's the only time he can rehearse, but can I cook you dinner next week? I'd like to continue this.

ELEANOR. What a very short date. Maybe the shortest date I've ever had.

BOBBY. I'm sorry. But I can't help it. Let's say Wednesday for dinner? I'm a decent cook. Nothing fancy. At seven? I really like talking to you.

ELEANOR. Just tell me exactly how fast I should eat on Wednesday.

BOBBY. Look, it just worked out this way. It's nothing personal. (*Gets up.*) In fact, I've been thinking about kissing you. I'd like to kiss you.

ELEANOR. Why do you want to kiss me if we're friends?

BOBBY. It's a friendly kiss.

ELEANOR. Okay. When?

BOBBY. Now. (*Stands up.*)

ELEANOR. In front of everyone? (*Stands up.*)

BOBBY. This is New York. If you can't do it here, you can't do it —

ELEANOR. Okay.

(BOBBY slowly approaches her and gives her a long, passionate kiss.)

ELEANOR. Oh. *(SHE backs off and staggers a little, surprised by the intensity of the kiss.)*
BOBBY. See you Wednesday.

(THEY FREEZE as THEY look at each other.)

BLACKOUT

Scene 2

Wednesday evening at Bobby's apartment.
AT RISE: ELEANOR, still dressed in all black, is sitting on the floor at a low coffee table sipping a glass of mineral water. There are two place settings and two glasses but no food on the table. Two unlit candles are also on the table.
A small bookcase is against the wall.
BOBBY lights a match and ignites the candle wicks.

BOBBY. You don't mind sitting on the floor?
ELEANOR. *(Shaking her head no.)* Uh-huh.
BOBBY. When I eat, I want to be relaxed. *(HE heads back towards the kitchen offstage.)*
ELEANOR. Great. I'm always worried whether I'm eating too fast. Someone once told me to chew thirty times and then swallow, but it gets so boring. And, of course, you can't have a conversation if you're counting.
BOBBY. Where do you get all this stuff you say?
ELEANOR. I don't know. What do you mean?
BOBBY. Why don't you just talk plain?
ELEANOR. Because when I was growing up my dad said not to talk to him unless I had something original to say, something

that wasn't trite, hackneyed, or banal. So I used to practice talking to myself in front of the mirror. My own talk show, you know. I held up canned goods for the commercial breaks — string beans, corn Niblets, cranberry sauce, like that.

BOBBY. (*Walks over to her holding two plates of spaghetti. HE gives her a long, serious look.*) Maybe you should think about therapy. It's really helping me.

ELEANOR. No thanks. Everyone I know is in therapy and they all give me advice. That's enough counselling for the entire Sioux Nation. If there still was one. And you know, everyone tells me something different. Alas!

BOBBY. There you go again. (*Puts plate in front of her.*)

ELEANOR. I can't help it.

BOBBY. You do it for attention, but you don't have to with me. I'm listening.

ELEANOR. I know. (*Looks down at plate.*) And look how elegantly you've placed the food on the plate. It has the serenity of a Japanese flower arrangement.

BOBBY. Now why are you making fun of me?

ELEANOR. I was trying to say thank you.

BOBBY. You don't have to. I like you.

ELEANOR. (*Pause.*) I loved the way you read that poem you left on my answering machine. It was so moving.

BOBBY. It was Keats. You know him?

ELEANOR. Uh-huh. (*Nodding affirmatively.*) Nobody ever read me a poem before.

BOBBY. I liked it so I wanted to share it with you. That's all.

ELEANOR. Very romantic.

(*Pause.*)

BOBBY. Hey. Is there something you expect me to say I'm not saying?

ELEANOR. I guess not. I suppose actors are more dramatic than other people. It's just the way they are.

BOBBY. I don't know about other actors. I act so I have my feelings. They're so stuck inside me it's hard to get them out. That poem expressed something.

ELEANOR. You did a great job with it. You're talented.

BOBBY. (*Goes to bookcase, chooses a book, opens it, and reads.*)

"And when I feel, fair creature of an hour!
That I shall never look upon thee more,
Never have relish in the faery power
Of unreflecting love! — then on the shore
Of the wide world I stand alone, and think
Till Love and Fame to nothingness do sink."

ELEANOR. That's when people believed in great love stories like Romeo and Juliet, and Cyrano de Bergerac. Now it's all downhill.

BOBBY. Kissing was the best part of our date.

ELEANOR. It was.

BOBBY. I liked kissing you.

ELEANOR. I liked it, too.

BOBBY. But I'm not kissing you again. I've been thinking about it. I want to be honest with you, and let you know this is not going to have a big finish.

ELEANOR. What do you mean?

BOBBY. I mean I'm attracted to you but I'm not going to bed with you. That's not where this is leading. I don't want you to misunderstand.

ELEANOR. I thought we were just in the getting to know each other phase.

BOBBY. Getting to know and you wanting a relationship.

ELEANOR. No. I don't know if I do.

BOBBY. You do. That's why we have to stay friends. I don't want to hurt you, and I will if we get involved. I'm trying to stop myself this time.

ELEANOR. Look, this is only our second date. I don't have any expectations. How can you go to the end of our relationship when we don't even have one?

BOBBY. Because whenever I try, I always get hurt, and hurt somebody else.

ELEANOR. So you're telling me. You're warning me.

BOBBY. That's why we have to stay friends. And why I can't kiss you anymore. This time it's not going to happen.

ELEANOR. You're a wonderful kisser, but all right.

BOBBY. Don't encourage me. I haven't finished working this all out in therapy, and I can see that you want to be hurt, but I don't want to hurt you.

ELEANOR. No. You're wrong. I don't want to be hurt. Why do you say that?

BOBBY. When I invited you to dinner, what did you think would happen?

ELEANOR. I thought we would eat dinner.

BOBBY. And then?

ELEANOR. I didn't know. I'd see.

BOBBY. You were going to repeat it. Repeat your pattern. I can tell about you. You told me men let you down. You choose them for that.

ELEANOR. No.

BOBBY. Well, this time it's not going to happen. I'm not giving you expectations. I'm not kissing you. Even though I liked it.

ELEANOR. I did, too.

BOBBY. Even though you'd still let me.

ELEANOR. Yes. I settle for so little. Isn't that sick?

BOBBY. I've been wondering if you're white all over. Your skin is so white.

ELEANOR. Because when I was eight, I went to the beach and burned my insteps. They carried me home, and I never went to the beach again. It's no fun swimming in a hat, a tee shirt, and socks. And I had to use an inner tube to stay afloat wearing all that, and everyone made so much fun of me, it wasn't worth it. Don't kiss me if you're going to hurt me.

BOBBY. (*Standing up.*) Time to go.

ELEANOR. Oh! Is there a second shift?

BOBBY. What's wrong?

ELEANOR. You decided you don't like me any more. (*Opens her hand bag, takes out a lipstick, and puts it on without looking. Then, puts the lipstick back and closes bag.*)

BOBBY. I do like you. I want to kiss you very much. That's why I think we should leave and I should walk you home instead.

ELEANOR. (*Upset.*) Okay.

BOBBY. Please. Believe me. I'm not kicking you out. I'm trying to do what's right. It's hard. That's why I have to take control like this.

ELEANOR. At least you can. I can't say even say "leave" to anyone. I just let them go.

BOBBY. I know. But I want to see you again. When are you inviting me to your place? (*Puts baseball cap on to leave.*)

ELEANOR. You like Chinese take-out?

BOBBY. Sounds good. When?

ELEANOR. I'm not sure.

BOBBY. Be brave. Pick a day. I'll say yes.

ELEANOR. Okay. Tuesday. Eight o'clock.

BOBBY. (*Starts towards door. Offers her his hand.*) I'll be there.

ELEANOR. (*Taking his hand.*) I bet your hair looks great even when you sleep.

BOBBY. I sleep naked.

ELEANOR. Me, too. But that's not what I meant.

BOBBY. It's okay. I understand.

ELEANOR. I've spent a lot of time talking to myself. Sometimes I just blurt out what I'm thinking, when I shouldn't.

BOBBY. In front of a mirror holding up cans so somebody would love you.

(*THEY walk to the door.*)

ELEANOR. I'd really like it if you were my friend.

BOBBY. (*Turns, and touches her shoulder with his free hand.*) I am.

(*THEY FREEZE as THEY look at each other.*)

BLACKOUT

Scene 3

Eleanor's apartment the following Tuesday.
AT RISE: ELEANOR, still dressed all in black, is taking cartons of
   Chinese food out of a bag and putting them on the table.
   BOBBY sprawls on the couch. HE is wearing a tight tee shirt
   and jeans.
There are books on a shelf against the wall.

ELEANOR. Egg roll. Chicken Chow Mein. Shrimp with
bamboo shoots. I didn't want to get too adventurous.

BOBBY. (*Grinning.*) You could have been adventurous.

ELEANOR. Well, I bought Passion Fruit drink. How about
that?

BOBBY. I prefer scotch.

ELEANOR. Oh. I didn't know you drank?

BOBBY. With ice. (*Lights a cigarette.*)

ELEANOR. You smoke, too?

BOBBY. I need one. I'm stopping but right now I'm not.

ELEANOR. (*Goes and gets ice and glasses. Hands him the*
bottle.) Are you okay? You seem different.

(*SHE sets the ice in front of him with the bottle. BOBBY pours*
   himself a giant drink)

ELEANOR. Wow! That's a tall one.

BOBBY. It's fine. You want some?

ELEANOR. No. Thanks. I have seltzer. Drinking slows my
mental processes down.

BOBBY. You don't have to worry about being intelligent for
me. Believe me, I'm not that smart. Really, I'm not very smart at
all.

ELEANOR. Why do you say that? You're perceptive. I've been
thinking about our dinner last week. What you said made a
difference.

BOBBY. Great. But right now I feel shitty. Last night acting class was a nightmare. I'm not connecting with the material. I feel hollow. Bottoms up. (*HE drinks, and then pours himself another.*)

ELEANOR. I'm sorry.

BOBBY. I need to believe in me. Believe my own belief. I think I'm a phoney.

ELEANOR. You're not. (*Portions out the Chinese food.*)

BOBBY. (*Looking at her.*) I miss kissing you.

ELEANOR. Why did you say that?

BOBBY. That's how I feel. (*Pours himself more scotch.*)

ELEANOR. Why are you saying that? What about our deal?

BOBBY. It doesn't mean I can't be attracted to you. That I don't want to explore our sexuality.

ELEANOR. (*Sits down next to him.*) What about our friendship?

BOBBY. It's different here. I'm under your influence.

ELEANOR. Believe me. I don't have any or I would have already been promoted at work. I've been in the contracts department too long. I should be in foreign rights by now.

BOBBY. (*Looking at her, lusting for her.*) Why did you invite me over here?

ELEANOR. We're being friends. You made me that great dinner. I'm reciprocating. Why are you acting like this?

BOBBY. I'm very attracted to you. Don't you feel that, too?

ELEANOR. (*Jumps up.*) I thought we were going to read poetry and get to know each other better. (*SHE grabs a pair of glasses and puts them on. Then goes over to book shelf, picks up a book, and reads.*) "Men seldom make passes at girls who wear glasses." That's Dorothy Parker. And look, I have Baudelaire, too.

BOBBY. Should I go? Ask me to go.

ELEANOR. No. Just don't drink any more. I don't want to ruin everything.

BOBBY. Tell me to go.

ELEANOR. You know I can't.

BOBBY. Tell me to go.

ELEANOR. You said you go to bed with women and hurt them because it never works out. I believe you.

BOBBY. (*Gets up, goes over to the book shelf, picks up a book, leafs through it until he finds what he is looking for, and then starts reading.*)

"And there it was I lived in pleasures calm,
Amid the splendours, heaven and the waves,
And perfume saturated, naked slaves,
Who gently soothed my brow with fronds of palm,
And whose unique concern was fathoming
The secret grief which left me languishing."

(*Pouring more to drink.*) Twice every Sunday and every Wednesday night at 7:30, I was dragged to church until when I was twenty-one I couldn't take it anymore. (*Pause.*) They made me ashamed to want the center of attention. I was supposed to sit in a corner and be nothing.

ELEANOR. You don't have to prove anything to me.

BOBBY. I have a right to be.

ELEANOR. You'll make it. You're talented.

BOBBY. (*Moving towards her.*) You want someone to protect you. Someone to take care of you. Someone who will be the answer to your problems. Someone you can hide behind.

ELEANOR. Why does that sound just like something you say to someone to convince them?

BOBBY. What are you accusing me of?

ELEANOR. I thought we were friends. (*Starts crying. HE moves towards her.*) Please. That's what I want. Friends. (*THEY hug.*)

BOBBY. You feel so good.

ELEANOR. You do, too.

(*Pause.*)

BOBBY. We should get comfortable. (*HE kisses her.*)

ELEANOR. We should talk. (*SHE kisses him back.*)

BOBBY. We can talk after.

(*THEY quickly tumble onto the couch as HE kisses her.*)

ELEANOR. Is this why you came over?

BOBBY. No. I didn't even think about it. It just happened.

ELEANOR. But could you — could you —

BOBBY. What?

ELEANOR. Be tender.

(*Pause.*)

BOBBY. Why did you say that?

ELEANOR. I don't know what happened. My feelings came out.

BOBBY. I can't do this. (*Stands up.*) There's nothing for me. It's empty.

ELEANOR. You frightened me. I don't want to be there alone. That's what hurts when it's over. (*Looks at him, says nothing, and gets up.*)

BOBBY. Don't act like that and walk away.

ELEANOR. How do you expect me to act? (*Goes and sits down in a corner on the floor holding her knees.*)

BOBBY. Okay. You're right. I wanted to use you, and I didn't want to communicate with you on any level at all. (*Pause.*) I feel terrible.

ELEANOR. I trusted you. (*SHE gets up and walks in the other direction.*)

BOBBY. I wanted the excitement and the heat.

ELEANOR. And my life?

BOBBY. Stop! Don't blame it all on me. You let me stay.

ELEANOR. I wanted you to stay but not like this.

BOBBY. I don't have anything to give right now. I like you but—

ELEANOR. Ironic, isn't it? It's the same old routine but this time I couldn't do it to myself, and because of you. Because of what you showed me. And then after all that, you still tried.

(*Pause.*)

BOBBY. I told you sex was my weakness. (*Holding stomach.*)

Ohh. My stomach. You made me think. I didn't want to think. I didn't figure this right.

ELEANOR. Don't you see? You couldn't go through with it either. Aren't you glad?

BOBBY. It's hard to change. (*Turns away. Starts putting his shirt on and gets ready to go.*)

ELEANOR. You're going?

BOBBY. I didn't have time to see you tonight, really. I was leaving early anyway. I have auditions tomorrow. There's a couple monologues I have to learn for class.

ELEANOR. When will I see you again?

BOBBY. (*Surprised.*) You want to? I don't know. I have a busy few weeks coming up.

ELEANOR. Oh.

BOBBY. Look, I'm doing the best I can. I don't feel very good about myself right now. I liked you. (*HE turns to leave.*)

ELEANOR. Wait! I get it. You've set this whole thing up to hurt yourself.

BOBBY. Yes.

(*Pause.*)

ELEANOR. But you also hurt me.

BOBBY. That's why we're together. Isn't it? That's how people like us get to feel. Isn't it? The pain is what we're used to.

ELEANOR. (*Walks over to him.*) No. Somebody has to stop it. You kept hurting each other for twelve years, didn't you? You and your girlfriend.

BOBBY. Honey, I don't want any of this relationship stuff. I can't handle it.

ELEANOR. No matter what you say, I'm not going to reject you. (*TANGO MUSIC slowly starts fading in.*) I'm not going to make you feel ashamed. That's your game but I'm not playing it with you.

BOBBY. You're just being kind, aren't you?

ELEANOR. No. I'm being your friend. That was our deal. I'm keeping my end of the bargain.

(BOBBY looks at her and shakes his head. The TANGO MUSIC gets louder.)

BOBBY. I'm sorry I put you through all this.

ELEANOR. I'm glad. *(Walks him to the door. HE stares hard at her.)* Don't you see? The weirdest thing just happened and my life will never be the same again. Doesn't that make you feel good? Is feeling good, so bad?

BOBBY. *(Looks at her again.)* I don't know what it is about you.

ELEANOR. Why?

BOBBY. *(Upset.)* I'm not worth it.

ELEANOR. Now I'm getting mad. *(The TANGO MUSIC gets louder.)* You did me a favor. Don't you understand?

BOBBY. *(Looks at her.)* You're crazy. You know that?

ELEANOR. No. I'm not crazy. And you don't have to be either. *(THEY look at one another.)* Try.

BOBBY. I don't know if I can. *(The TANGO MUSIC increases in volume.)*

ELEANOR. You only have to want to.

BOBBY. I can't believe I'm doing this. *(HE walks towards her.)*

ELEANOR. Can't believe what?

BOBBY. Eleanor, I'm dipping you.

(In a slow pantomime, SHE holds her hand out to him. HE takes it, puts his other arm around her waist, and bends her backwards. THEY FREEZE as the TANGO music plays on. The LIGHTS fade.)

THE END

COSTUME PLOT

Scene 1
ELEANOR: black sweater, black mini skirt, black tights, black shoes
BOBBY: jeans, a blue shirt. casual jacket

Scene 2
ELEANOR: black sweater, black pants, black shoes, black jacket
BOBBY: jeans, a white shirt, baseball cap, casual jacket

Scene 3
ELEANOR: demure black sweater, black mini skirt, black fishnet tights, black shoes
BOBBY: tight white tee shirt, jeans, casual jacket

PROPERTY PLOT

Scene 1
a table, 2 chairs, plastic menu, coffee mug and spoon, handbag, a
  piece of junk mail

Scene 2
low coffee table, 2 candles in candle holders, 2 plates of spaghetti,
  2 forks, 2 napkins, 1 glass, a book of matches, two cushions, a
  couch, a small bookcase

Scene 3
couch, a book shelf, a brown paper bag, two Chinese food cartons,
  two sets of chop sticks, two plates, two glasses, a side table, a
  table, a tablecloth, a bottle of scotch, a bottle of mineral water, a
  package of cigarettes, matches, an ashtray, Tango music

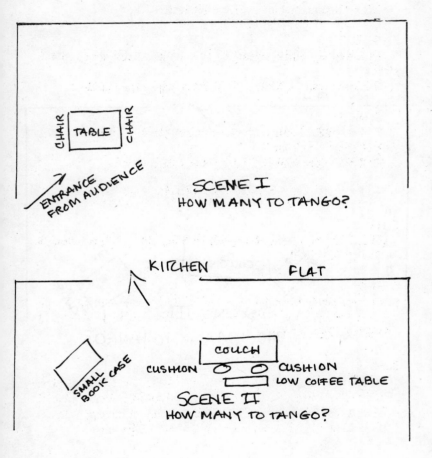

CHAIR TABLE CHAIR

ENTRANCE FROM AUDIENCE

SCENE I
HOW MANY TO TANGO?

KITCHEN   FLAT

SMALL BOOK CASE   CUSHION   COUCH   CUSHION
                                      LOW COFFEE TABLE

SCENE II
HOW MANY TO TANGO?

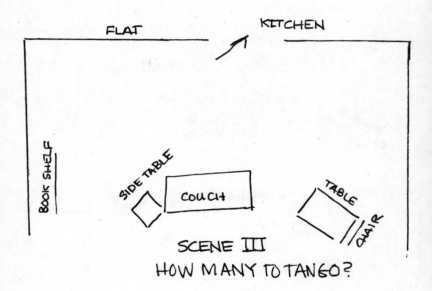

FLAT　　　　　　KITCHEN

BOOK SHELF

SIDE TABLE　COUCH　TABLE　CHAIR

SCENE III
HOW MANY TO TANGO?

VISITING OLIVER

a play in one act

by Bill Nave

for Paula Jean Ewin,
always an inspiration,
and for
Carol Kulikowski,
who first introduced me to
Ruth

Visiting Oliver premiered at the 18th Annual Off-Off Broadway Festival of Plays. It was presented by The 29th Street Repertory Theatre, Inc., Tim Corcoran, Artistic Director, with the following cast:

RUTH..Paula Ewin

CLEMENT ....Leo Farley

OLIVER ....David Mogentale

STANLEY...Ted Osborne

Directed by Vera Beren
Lighting by Stewart Wagner
Sound by Robert Derby/Vera Beren

CHARACTERS

RUTH — She is solid as the earth and proud — even though her clothes are rather worn and are probably safety-pinned together. In her middle forties, she is a woman who has worked hard her entire life. Finding it increasingly difficult to keep her optimism and certain faith, she does, nonetheless, still fight to claim them.

CLEMENT — A brooding and intense young man in the first year of recovery from alcoholism. He reeks of insolence and Old Spice.

OLIVER — A big man with an even bigger heart. He wears a lop-sided grin but is far from "cute." He has huge hands and feet and is rather good humored, though he has a tendency to darkness, as well, that surfaces in surprising moments.

STAN — One of the other residents, he is sickly, pale and has slicked hair that sticks to his skull. Even though he is confined to his wheelchair, and has no use of his body, we get the feeling that he is fully aware of his predicament.

TIME & PLACE

The action of the play takes place in the visitor's room of the New Beulah Home for the Mentally Incapacitated, just outside of Hopkinsville, Kentucky.

A recent summer.

VISITING OLIVER

*In the DARKNESS, a match flares and a cigarette is lit. MUSIC
and LIGHTS rise simultaneously.*
*RUTH stands in a beam of blinding light far upstage. SHE walks
slowly towards us.*

RUTH. I am Ruth. From the size of me, you'd never believe
what's in here. But a lot, a lot. I'm a strong enough woman. Oncet
carried a chest of drawers down seven flights of stairs by myself.
The drawers were empty, of course, but, still, a chest of drawers is
a chest of drawers. I'm brave enough too, I reckon. Hard winters.
A rat come up in the yard oncet, showing ugly brown teeth. I killed
that rat. Beat him down to such a stinking pulp the neighbors had
to ask what that was a carcass of. I had eight children, all told,
starting with Oliver when I was just slipping past fourteen. Most of
them got through their early days in one piece, or near enough. The
second one died when she was only two years old. Run over by the
milk cart. The Devil draws children and poodles to the road and
God himself, it seems, can't stop that lure. But, Oliver, Oliver.
Doctors all told me it weren't my fault how he come to be. A boy
with no hope. Still, a mother's heart can take on burdens no other
heart can know. I am Ruth. And I am dying. That's why I'm
visiting Oliver.

*(SOUNDS of a lush and happy summer in the distance: a lawn
    mower, birds, a dog. RUTH enters the waiting area. SHE grips
    firmly a large fruit basket wrapped brilliantly in yards of
    colored cellophane. A shiny red purse hangs off her arm.*
*CLEMENT is oblivious to her. HE smokes a cigarette as if his life
    depended on it. HE has greased hair, mirrored sunglasses and
    plenty of attitude. HE is dressed in an orderly's uniform. As the
    MUSIC fades away, RUTH clears her throat. Again. HE
    doesn't flinch.)*

RUTH. I'm sorry. Young man. I'm sorry.

(HE looks at her. SHE squints at her reflection in his shades, straightening her hair.)

RUTH. Thank you. There's not a mirror in the ladies' room.

CLEMENT. I ain't the janitor. Tell him.

RUTH. Well, now, I didn't think you were.

CLEMENT. I'm dressed like this 'cause I'm an orderly. I don't got nothing to do with no mirror in no ladies' room.

RUTH. I'm seeing my son today. Today, right?

CLEMENT. I tell you I'll fetch him when I'm done my break. Do I look like I'm done my break?

RUTH. My hair look okay?

(CLEMENT throws down his cigarette, crushes it out, walks across the room and bends down until his glasses are just inches from her eyes. SHE smiles at her reflection nervously.)

RUTH. It's my son, you see. I want to. So shiny. You use Windex?

CLEMENT. Vinegar and water.

RUTH. You don't! Didn't think young people nowadays knew that trick. And dry with newspaper. I *am* a janitor. Sometimes. Take in cleaning. Sweep hair up at the beauty shop. Wrap packages. Defrost refrigerators. I go all the time. Scrape together what I can.

CLEMENT. Busy lady.

RUTH. Oh, yes! But it keeps the pain at bay.

CLEMENT. Too busy to see your boy, I reckon.

RUTH. Beg pardon?

CLEMENT. He been in here how long and you ain't been here once?

RUTH. I been here.

CLEMENT. Not since I been on and that's been nine years?

RUTH. After I brought him. I came once then.

CLEMENT. Hell, lady, he's an old man now.

RUTH. Hardly *old*.

CLEMENT. The other side of thirty, if he's a day. When'd you dump him?

RUTH. I didn't dump him. There was no hope. He was a boy of no hope. Check his file. I bet those very words are in there still.

CLEMENT. Oliver's a sweetie. You're the one, got no hope. Your doctors are the ones, got no hope. You all are the ones what should be locked up in here, not him. Not Oliver.

RUTH. Is your break over yet?

CLEMENT. (*Lighting another Camel.*) I'll worry about my break. You people on the outside, driving up in your cars. A minute you think you'll give your crazy kin. They don't need you. They don't need your minute.

RUTH. I did not come in no car. I walked up the drive. I saved for the bus here. I'm sleeping in Motel Six on the highway. So, I don't need no smart mouthed boy who wears too much after shave to give me grief! I got grief enough for my own! (*Visibly shaken.*) Look, all I want's my son. *Please.*

(*CLEMENT doesn't move.*)

RUTH. I'll go out there myself and —

CLEMENT. And find him yourself? You'd look a sight running down the halls, yelling for the long lost lamb! What was it finally got your ass in here? Most people don't come till they're dying.

(*SHE stands in fury, her eyes roll up in the back of her head, SHE moans and falls back down.*)

CLEMENT. I'm sorry. Lady. Lady. Look. Don't take it so. Hey. You all right? Lady? (*HE goes to check her pulse, looks in her eyes.*) Jesus, oh, sweet Jesus. Look, I'm not a doctor, lady. I'm just an orderly. Don't do this. Hey, hey, lady. Mrs. Waller. Mrs. Waller, can you hear me?

RUTH. (*Faint as a ripple of water.*) Yes. Yes. I can. Yes.

CLEMENT. I'm fetching the doctor.

RUTH. NO! I didn't come here for doctors.

CLEMENT. Something's wrong.

RUTH. Just a heart that's breaking.

CLEMENT. I didn't mean to rag on you so much.

RUTH. It takes more than some smart aleck *orderly* to do me in. I am Ruth Waller. I been through more.

CLEMENT. Some water?

RUTH. Please.

(SHE takes some pills, puts them under her tongue and HE sees this as HE hands her a cup of water.)

RUTH. Thank you.

CLEMENT. You a diabetic or something?

RUTH. Something.

CLEMENT. I am. A diabetic. Alcoholic diabetic. Not a good combination. But a common one.

RUTH. They got a diabetic watching my son?

CLEMENT. It's not contagious.

RUTH. I meant alcoholic. They got an alcoholic attending my son?

CLEMENT. In recovery.

RUTH. Which means?

CLEMENT. I don't steal drugs from the nurse's station no more.

RUTH. No more.

CLEMENT. I'm lucky. Got caught. Got shipped to this alcoholic rehabilitation center. And now I'm back on probation. I love New Beulah. My boys. But if you was to have a full blown seizure, conk out on me, it wouldn't look good on my record.

RUTH. So get me my boy. I can't promise anything.

CLEMENT. I was going to. I'll send him right along. My break's —

RUTH. I know. Your break. It's over.

(HE exits. SHE shakes her head. Mops the sweat away. Drinks more water. Looks around.)

RUTH. This room. I want to remember this room, Oliver. Keep it in my little jewelry box. (*SHE closes her eyes tightly, memorizing.*) Sea foam green walls. Red and black checkerboard linoleum. Soda machine. (Out of Dr. Pepper.) Water cooler. Cigarette machine. Dog-ear magazines. Ripped chair. Foam stuffing. Dying spider plant. Venetian blinds. Dirty windows. Yellow sunlight. Dust in the sunlight.

(*A MAN appears in the doorway. SHE senses this and opens her eyes.*)

RUTH. And Oliver. The spitting image of your father.
OLIVER. Hello there.
RUTH. Hello there. You don't remember me, I know. No reason you should. Why would you?
OLIVER. I remember you.
RUTH. Really?
OLIVER. The way you smell. I remember you always smelled good.
RUTH. You don't remember me. I smelled like a work horse. (*HE whinnies.*) My whole life, just a work horse.
OLIVER Horses smell good. I know. The Shriners bring a circus here every year. I ride a pony. Cows are good, too. They don't bring no cows. You look pretty.
RUTH. (*Her hands nervously flutter over her hair.*) No, no. My hair.
OLIVER. You combed out your hair. At night. In front of a mirror.
RUTH. In front of the window. Not very pretty now, what's left of it. Your mother, she's having treatments done and it's. Well. So darned hard on the hair.
OLIVER. Crowning glory.
RUTH. Beg pardon?
OLIVER. The Bible says a woman's hair is her crowning glory.
RUTH. They read you from the Bible here? That's real nice.
OLIVER. You read us stories from the Bible.

RUTH. You couldn't have been more than four at the most, Oliver.

OLIVER. I love you.

RUTH. I took the bus here.

OLIVER. I love you.

RUTH. Greyhound. Greyhound bus.

OLIVER. You are the prettiest mother I ever seen come in here.

RUTH. With the dog on the side? You used to love puppies.

OLIVER. Ruff! Ruff! Ruff!

RUTH. We had puppies. You remember?

OLIVER. RUFF! RUFF! RUFF!

RUTH. Oliver, they'll come in and check on us if we're not good.

OLIVER. What kinda dog we have?

RUTH. Ugly kinda dog. You loved him, though. He loved you. You pulled him around by his ears and, still, he loved you.

OLIVER. Like Daddy?

RUTH. Like Daddy?

OLIVER. Pulled you around by your ears and you still loved him.

RUTH. After all he did to you, looks like you could block him out.

OLIVER. Oh, no. I love Daddy.

RUTH. He was an awful man.

OLIVER. He was a shit.

RUTH. He was your father.

OLIVER. I loved him.

RUTH. I left him. After you were hurt. Did you know that?

OLIVER. I'm glad. I am. He was a shit.

RUTH. They let you talk like that in here?

OLIVER. I talk like I want.

RUTH. You just had a birthday, Oliver.

OLIVER. I know. The doctors say I'm nine now.

RUTH. You look good.

OLIVER. I think I'm big for nine.

RUTH. The people on your daddy's side was all on the big side. You take after them.

OLIVER. I don't take after you.

RUTH. Maybe a little.

OLIVER. No! You're a tiny little thing. Tiny, tiny parakeet. I could squash you in my hands.

RUTH. My head, honey, my head. You don't want to do that!

OLIVER. No. You're strong.

RUTH. That's right.

OLIVER. You want to wrestle? They'll let us wrestle but we have to put the mats away and we can't bet any money.

RUTH. Your mother's not feeling very well these days, Oliver.

OLIVER. Then we won't wrestle *hard*.

(*HE lifts her in his arms above his head. SHE closes her eyes and pats his arm nervously.*)

OLIVER. Where's your car? Will you show me your car later? I can drive. I watch movies and that's where I learned to drive. You're busting me out of here.

RUTH. I don't have a car, Oliver. I don't have enough money for a car. I had to save for a bus ticket here. You live very far away from me and I am not well and I wanted to see you before it got too late. Now put your mother down.

OLIVER. You don't want to be up there?

RUTH. Enough for today.

OLIVER. We can put mud on your feet and I will walk you across the ceiling and then when they come in to take me away, they will see footprints across the ceiling and they will wonder how they got up there and we will look away and act like we don't have any idea how they got up there.

RUTH. Maybe on my next visit.

OLIVER. (*Puts her down.*) You won't visit me again.

RUTH. Of course I will.

OLIVER. NO!

RUTH. Shh! They'll think I'm hurting you. I brought you some goodies. Now sit down and you be good and I'll give them to you, all right?

OLIVER. You love me?

RUTH. Oh, Oliver.

OLIVER. I often wonder, if I was okay, would you and Daddy have loved me more?

RUTH. There is nothing wrong with you, Oliver.

OLIVER. Then why am I in the New Beulah Home for the Mentally Incapacitated just outside of Hopkinsville, Kentucky?

RUTH. Because there are people here who can love you better than your mother, and certainly your father, ever could.

OLIVER. Would you have loved me more if there wasn't something wrong with me?

RUTH. I love you just the way you are, Oliver.

OLIVER. All right. Would you have *visited* me more if there wasn't something wrong with me?

RUTH. When I called up last week, they said you liked fruit. Look what I brought you.

OLIVER. (*Lackluster.*) Oh, boy. Fruit.

RUTH. A deluxe fruit basket. You can keep the basket when the fruit is gone.

OLIVER. Thank you so much. Do you have any cigarettes?

RUTH. You smoke?

OLIVER. I know I'm still a minor but you don't have to worry about it stunting my growth.

RUTH. I can't believe they let you smoke.

OLIVER. Do you smoke after sex?

RUTH. Oliver!

OLIVER. Answer! Answer!

RUTH. I most certainly will not.

OLIVER. No, you say. No! And then you say to me, "Do you?" Go ahead. "Do you?"

RUTH. I am still your mother.

OLIVER. And then I say, "I don't know, I never looked." Get it?

RUTH. I can't believe they let you smoke. That drunk is not a good influence.

OLIVER. Thanks for the fruit.

RUTH. You're welcome.

OLIVER. But I don't really like fruit.

RUTH. I wish they'd told me. I wouldn't have spent — I'd have gotten something you liked.

OLIVER. A carton of Camels.

RUTH. And something that was *good* for you. You like candy?

OLIVER. Chocolate.

RUTH. I would've gotten you Goobers, then.

OLIVER. How is everybody.

RUTH. Everybody is fine.

OLIVER. Anybody say to say "hi" to me or anything?

RUTH. Nobody knows you're here. Nobody knows *I'm* here. Nobody knows I was coming.

OLIVER. You just disappeared?

RUTH. Yes.

OLIVER. Watch out. You'll be on TV and everybody will be looking for you.

RUTH. I'll be back before they even miss me, Oliver. You don't have to be in New Beulah for you to feel lonely and locked away. I don't get many visitors myself.

OLIVER. Yeah, but you have a choice don't you?

RUTH. I suppose I do.

OLIVER. I like visitors. Sometimes, on Sundays, when churches come, I just pretend that those people are here to see me.

RUTH. Why, I'm sure they are.

OLIVER. No. They're here to see other people. Not me. There's this one preacher, though. He makes beautiful animals out of balloons. You want me to show you?

RUTH. I don't have any balloons, I'm afraid.

OLIVER. Don't be afraid. These animals can't hurt you. Watch. *(HE pulls balloons from his pocket. HE blows them up and very expertly ties one into a dog.)* See?

RUTH. Oh that's wonderful!

OLIVER. It's a dog.

RUTH. Why, it certainly is. A beautiful little weiner dog.

OLIVER. You really like it?

RUTH. It's just splendid.

OLIVER. Take it.

RUTH. I couldn't.

OLIVER. You hate it.

RUTH. I do not.

OLIVER. Then why are you crying?

RUTH. Balloons don't last.

OLIVER. Neither do flowers. Neither do we. Nothing lasts. Sing to me.

RUTH. My voice is still the same.

OLIVER. Sweetest voice because it's my mama's. Sing to me.

RUTH. Darlin'.

OLIVER. Please?

RUTH. What would you like?

OLIVER. My favorite.

RUTH. You pick.

OLIVER. No, you.

RUTH. (*Singing.*) I went to the Animal Fair ...

OLIVER. Wait, wait!

(*OLIVER crawls up in RUTH's lap. Nestles. His legs and arms drape luxuriously over her tiny frame. The tableau is rather like the Pieta — seen in a fun house mirror. RUTH is so stunned she cannot speak, much less sing.*)

OLIVER. Well? Go on. Go on.

RUTH. (*Singing.*) "I went to the animal fair, the birds and the bees were there ...

OLIVER. My hair.

RUTH. What?

OLIVER. Run your fingers through my hair.

RUTH. (*SHE does.*) "The big baboon by the light of the moon, was combing his auburn hair. The monkey he got drunk. He fell on the elephant's trunk. The elephant sneezed and fell to his knees and that was the end of the monk!"

OLIVER. *Kerplunk!*

RUTH. *Kerplunk!*

RUTH. You have a good voice. You sound like your daddy. He had a good voice. I hand that much to him.

OLIVER. You still see him?

RUTH. I left him right after the incident. I wish I could be sorry. I'm not.

OLIVER. No?

RUTH. No. He was a shit. I am sorry that I stayed with him as long as I did. They didn't have talk shows in my time like they got nowadays on the TV. If they had, I would've known it was all right to leave him. That just because you swear to stick by somebody for better or worse — and *this* in the presence of God — that those are just words and you aren't really held accountable for what you say anymore. It's all just words now. He was mean. He was drunk. And if I had left him when I should've, you might not be in here today and for that I am so sorry. Do you understand?

OLIVER. (*Really trying.*) You would've loved me more if you'd left him earlier.

RUTH. The night I did leave him, carrying that chest of drawers out of the apartment, where I got the strength I don't know, he threw you against that chest of drawers. The back of your head. It was. I am so sorry. You still have that scar?

OLIVER. I never look. It's on the back of my head.

RUTH. So, I let them put you in here and I try to deal with that awful mess. And the way I deal with it is to not see you for twenty-seven years. And that's why I've brought you the deluxe fruit basket. And these comics. And this roll of quarters.

OLIVER. QUARTERS!

RUTH. For your soda machine. They said they let you have sodas on Thursdays.

OLIVER. All these for me?

RUTH. All for you.

(*HE takes them and sits on the floor and opens the roll and makes little piles with them.*)

RUTH. All for you. My baby. Can you keep a secret, Oliver? Oh, your mama's just *full* of secrets. You got a whole mess of stepsisters and brothers and a nice stepdaddy who don't know a smidge about you. I locked all that away. I'm sorry. If it had happened now, I might have known better. In those days we locked people up when there was no hope. You are so much better now. You are so much better than when I brought you in here. You're better off, frankly, than the grandchildren. You have six nephews and eight nieces, Oliver. Be thankful children aren't allowed up here. That's all I can say. Smart mouths. Children aren't grateful anymore. No one is. Nothing's left of the world except loud, awful music. Everybody's jumpy now, too, and it all goes, too, too fast. There's no hope. No faith. Things were always bad for your mother; a life spent on my knees, scraping pennies. But I always managed to believe things would get better, you know? It's just as well your mother is going now, before the world changes so much I don't even know her anymore. Oliver. Your mother has bad days now. Today, she's better than normal. (*With wonder and awe:*) But sometimes she'll be at the store and someone will be talking to her and she won't be able to see. And then when she does see, there are wheels of color, these greenish, glowing cauliflower heads, that's the only way I'm able to try and tell you what it's like, and purple lights. Your mother's got this little spot pressing in on her brain, getting bigger every day. And do you know what, darling? Darling?

OLIVER. What?

RUTH. Out of all my children, you're the only one I've been able to tell.

OLIVER. Thank you. Oh, how I love you.

RUTH. I. I.

OLIVER. Quarters!

RUTH. Quarters, yes, darlin', quarters.

(*CLEMENT comes on backwards with a wheelchair. In it sits a MAN in similar attire as OLIVER. Truly, though, a boy with no hope. His gaze is vacant. His hands are limp in his lap.*)

OLIVER. Look! Quarters!

RUTH. (*Wiping her eyes.*) Hello.

OLIVER. Look!

RUTH. Company. One of your little friends?

OLIVER. (*Whispering.*) Stanley. Stan for short.

*(RUTH is feeling rather chipper now and SHE takes one of his
  hands in hers.)*

RUTH. Hello, there. I'm Oliver's mother.

CLEMENT. Sorry it took so long. We had a little accident,
didn't we, boy?

RUTH. We've been having a wonderful visit. Thank you so
much.

CLEMENT. Good. He's all cleaned up now and just smelling
like a baby. He loves Johnson's Baby Powder, don't you boy?
Hope he hasn't been much trouble for you, ma'am. The three
o'clock girls been looking for you, Stan. Medication.

OLIVER. I have decided I'm not taking it this week.

CLEMENT. Oh, ho, you're not? You'll be picking people up
again, if we're not careful.

RUTH. Picking people up?

CLEMENT. When he gets excited.

OLIVER. Look, Clement. Quarters. And fruit. I'll trade you for
cigarettes.

CLEMENT. That's all nice. You put them back. I'm sure Mrs.
Waller didn't come all this way to give them to you. You don't
even like fruit.

OLIVER. She give 'em to me.

CLEMENT. You did?

RUTH. I did. I gave them. I did. I gave them to. This isn't
Oliver?

CLEMENT. Oliver? I told you. We had a little accident. Had to
change his dappers. Powder him. I hurried. I knew.

RUTH. *(Pointing to the boy in the wheelchair.) This* is Oliver?

CLEMENT. That's our boy. I told you he's a sweetie. Ain't he
a sweetie?

RUTH. Oh, sweet Jesus.

OLIVER. How many cigarettes can I buy with these?

CLEMENT. A few packs. Now come on, Stan, and leave Mrs.
Waller some time with alone with her son.

(HE stands, goes and kisses Ruth on the head.)

OLIVER. Thank you. I love you. And that was the end of the monk. *And that was the end of the monk!* Hey, you're supposed to sing back to me.

CLEMENT. Stanley, no trouble now. Don't wear out your welcome. Come on.

(CLEMENT goes out and STANLEY turns to follow. RUTH throws herself after him, screaming and attacking his back with ferocity.)

RUTH. Give me back my quarters you goddamn son of a bitch!

(OLIVER, in the wheelchair cries out as STANLEY falls to his knees and quarters and fruit roll everywhere.)

RUTH. You goddamn, goddamn son of a bitch!

(STANLEY is lying on the floor rolling back and forth, trying to protect himself and crying out in fear as RUTH vents her anger. CLEMENT comes rushing back in.)

CLEMENT. *(Overlapping.)* What the — ? Lady, hey! What the— Get off of — Hey, you want me to call security? Lady. Mrs. Waller.

RUTH. *(Overlapping.)* He stole my goddamn quarters. My goddamn ... He stole my ... Everything ... and that fruit basket. Deluxe ... You know ... Cost me. Cost me ... He ripped the cellophane ... he ripped ...

(SHE is heaving now. RUTH sobs. STANLEY sobs. OLIVER, in his wheelchair, sobs.)

RUTH. I just want my quarters back.

CLEMENT. *(Overlapping.)* It's okay, Stan. There, there fella. They're sick out there, too, honey. Shh. It's okay. Jesus Christ,

lady. You got some balls coming on my wing stirring up trouble.
You're out of here.

RUTH. But my son!

CLEMENT. You're out of here.

RUTH. I haven't gotten to see my son!

CLEMENT. I'm getting this one down to the nurse's station.
He's bleeding, Jesus! I'm back in ten for Oliver. If he's still crying
then, you're history. You are thrown away. Got it?

(CLEMENT exits comforting a confused and disoriented
STANLEY. RUTH looks after them. SHE picks up the quarters.
Finally, SHE picks herself up off the floor. She looks at Oliver.
HE is whimpering slightly, still looking straight ahead.)

RUTH. I'm sorry. I'm sorry. I'm sorry. There was so much I
wanted to tell you. So much I wanted you to know. Please don't be
scared of me. I couldn't bear it if you were scared of me. (SHE
crosses behind him, looks at the back of his skull. SHE touches the
scar gently and his keening grows louder.) Shh. Shh. I won't hurt
you anymore. I promise. I promise. Look. I brought you comics.
And fruit. And quarters for the soda machine. Would you like a
soda? That would be nice, wouldn't it?

(HE stops crying. SHE goes and gets him a soda.)

RUTH. I know it's not Thursday, but it'll be our little secret.
You need a straw, don't you, boy? There we go. Royal Crown.
You like that? They said you liked cola. Isn't that good?

(After an initial timidness, OLIVER greedily sucks down the black
nectar, still looking vacantly ahead. RUTH sits down next to
him, watches him drink. SHE smiles weakly.)

RUTH. That's it. That's my boy. Mama'll sit right here, and
we'll have us a nice, nice visit.

(HE finishes his soda. SHE wipes his mouth. SHE looks down at *her hands. Then SHE sees the balloon dog on the seat next to her. SHE lifts it, fondles it gently. SHE turns and smiles at Oliver as bravely as she is able and then SHE, too, stares ahead so that, when the LIGHTS fade down on the two of them, THEY both seem to be pondering the same view. Outside, a BIRD sings.)*

CURTAIN

COSTUME PLOT

RUTH
Brown wig (ill fitting)
Brown & beige
checked dress
Faded pale blue rain
coat
Beige shoes, low
heels
Shiny red purse

CLEMENT
Orderly whites
Black shoes
Photo i.d. tag
Sunglasses with
mirror shades

OLIVER
Dull-colored shirt
(green, blue)
Khaki trousers (too
short)
Cheap brown shoes or
old sneakers
Black (or white)
nylon socks
Black plastic belt

STANLEY
Dressed similarly to
Oliver

PROPERTIES LIST

<u>RUTH</u>
Gum
Rosary
Cigarettes
Lighter
Roll of quarters
Stack of comic books (tied)
Deluxe fruit basket wrapped in cellophane

<u>CLEMENT</u>
Cigarettes
Lighter
Smelling salts

<u>OLIVER</u>
Comb (in his back pocket)
Handkerchief
Balloons (several—in case one pops!)

SET DESIGN

In the original production, the stage was bare except for a long, low wooden bench set at a slight angle approximately stage center. Of course, in such a minimal production, the lighting took on an even more important role than usual; the designer, Stewart Wagner, used brighter, harsher lighting at the beginning of the play, opting for a dimmer, gentler look when Oliver enters, reverting to the brighter lighting upon Clement's return. This was a subtle but extremely powerful device. The lights also isolated the play's ending tableau, so that the two characters seemed to float together in a large dark void—this echoed the opening of the play when Ruth's monologue was spoken on a blue-and-purple-shadowed stage, the actress in silhouette until she drew nearer to the audience, stepping suddenly, and wonderfully, into golden light.

Bill Nave

Bill Nave, son of a Southern Baptist minister, is an eighth-generation Kentuckian who lives in Manhattan. He is the author of, among other plays, *NECKTIE BREAKFAST*, an epic twenty-two character play about the last public execution in the United States. It was produced at The 29th Street Repertory Theatre and Off-Broadway at the Harold Clurman Theatre. Also produced at The 29th Street Rep. was his play, *WITH SPIRIT AND WITH FIRE*. He has just completed three full-length plays: *WALKING ON WATER, WHAT THEY DID WITH HEARTS IN ROME*, and *BIBLE BURLESQUE with the words of Our Lord in red.*

THE POWER AND THE GLORY

by Le Wilhelm

Dedicated to

Sharon Fallon, Tracy Newirth, Diane Hoblit, Jeffrey Albright, Philip Galbraith, Sydney Russel

The Power and The Glory was originally produced under the title *Windows of the World* in spring of 1987 at the Cubiculo Theatre in New York City by Love Creek Productions. It was directed by Diane Hoblit with the following cast:

INEZ ....Lissa Watson

WANDA ....Anicia Ross

The play was again produced in 1990 with Ms. Hoblit directing the following cast:

INEZ ....Lissa Watson

WANDA ....Kate Zahorsky

In 1992 with revisions and a new title — *The Power and The Glory* was produced by Love Creek Productions, Artistic Director Philip Galbraith. Diane Hoblit directed the following cast:

INEZ ....Merry Beamer

WANDA ....CaSandra Brooks

CHARACTERS

INEZ — a woman somewhere between 19 and death

WANDA — a woman somewhere between 18 and one year before death

SETTING

A glass elevator, in a city.

The Power and The Glory

INEZ, a fairly attractive woman with a great amount of spirit, and WANDA, a shy woman.

INEZ. Now calm down, Wanda.

WANDA. I hate elevators.

INEZ. It's going to be worth it. You'll see.

WANDA. I don't know what you're trying to get me into, Inez. This is silly.

INEZ. You just wait, Wanda. It's going to help you. I do it whenever I get to feeling depressed and unwanted.

WANDA. It's going to make me sick. I hate elevators, and glass elevators are worse. I'll get sick and puke all over everything.

INEZ. No, you won't. You'll get over it in a minute.

WANDA. Don't be so sure.

INEZ. Enjoy the view.

WANDA. Inez, I don't see the point.

INEZ. The point is you're burned out, Wanda. You're burned out from waiting tables. You're depressed because of your love life, and you're going around like life is a Grade B horror movie. That's the point, Wanda. Now enjoy yourself as we go up. Isn't the view wonderful? Look, Wanda, everyone's getting smaller and smaller down there. So small like armies of little insects. Insects from all over the world. Down there on the street, insects from all over America, from all around the world. They're all down there, Wanda.

WANDA. I just don't like heights.

INEZ. You're going to learn to love them.

WANDA. I doubt that. This just scares me to death. Oh, God. We're moving faster.

INEZ. Look how small everyone is becoming —

WANDA. Faster and faster. What if we shoot through the roof?

INEZ. Metaphysically, we're going to shoot much higher than

the roof, Wanda.

WANDA. I don't see how this is going to cure my depression. I'm just not attractive to men. Men don't want me. I'm doomed to be an old maid.

INEZ. No, you're not. You're talking crazy.

WANDA. I'm unattractive and crazy. I don't know how I let you talk me into this.

INEZ. Well, it's too late now.

WANDA. Oh, dear God!

INEZ. You're going to thank your lucky stars I taught you this little trick. I know how you feel. It hit me early, when I first got here. I felt like a real loser. And then there was this girl I met from Toronto who showed me this. Now when I get to feeling unloved, unwanted, unattractive, I take a ride on the glass elevator. (*In a reprimanding voice.*) Wanda, it's important to look at the people down there. Now look!

WANDA. They're getting smaller and smaller.

INEZ. So small. But we remain large. Wanda, you have got to realize you're a beautiful woman, and all life springs from you.

WANDA. I'm not a mother.

INEZ. All life comes from woman. The human race survives because of us. We are the givers of life. If it weren't for us, there wouldn't be a human race.

WANDA. Feminist thought teaches us not to think of ourselves just as baby machines.

INEZ. I'm not talking about having kids. I'm talking about power.

WANDA. Oh, God. We're so high up. (*Looks away from below.*)

INEZ. Look down there.

WANDA. I can't.

INEZ. Yes, you can. Just take your time. We'll just push the hold button. Now, look down there, Wanda. It's important. Look. There you go.

WANDA. It's so far down.

INEZ. Yes, so far down. See all those little insect people down there.

WANDA. So small.

INEZ. Hundreds of men down there. Men of all races. Men from all over. Hundreds of men.

WANDA. There are women, too.

INEZ. We don't care about the women. Just the men. And there's hundreds of them.

WANDA. And not one wants me.

INEZ. Wrong. Look again, Wanda.

WANDA. I see them, Inez.

INEZ. Now did you do like I told you?

WANDA. Yes.

INEZ. You're not wearing any underwear and no pantyhose, right?

WANDA. No, I'm not, but I think that's the craziest thing I ever heard of. I was afraid to sit down on the subway. Going around in a skirt without panties on — I think you're making a fool out of me.

INEZ. I'm not wearing any, either.

WANDA. Maybe you are and maybe you're not.

INEZ. I'll show you.

WANDA. I believe you, Inez. Goodness.

INEZ. Now look close at those men down there, Wanda. What are they doing?

WANDA. They're going about their jobs, going to work, going to stores. I don't know what all of them are doing. Just walking around.

INEZ. No, Wanda.

WANDA. What are they doing?

INEZ. They're slowing down, Wanda. They're barely moving. They're almost at a standstill. Do you know why?

WANDA. They're waiting for the light to change?

INEZ. No, Wanda. They're looking up our dresses.

WANDA. (*Grabbing and tucking.*) They're what???

INEZ. They're looking up our dresses. That's why we didn't wear any underwear.

WANDA. That's dirty, Inez!!

INEZ. It's life, Wanda.

WANDA. They can't see anything this far up.

INEZ. Wrong, Wanda. When men are looking up women's dresses, their eyes are like those of an eagle.

WANDA. Oh, for goodness sake!

INEZ. They are. Stand a little closer to the glass, Wanda. Lift your skirt a little, spread your legs, let them see all the way up your dress.

WANDA. I most certainly will not!! Lord knows what kind of men are down there!

INEZ. All kinds of men. All kinds of men from all over the world. The rich, the poor, the religious, the infidels. The lovers, the haters, they're all there, and now (*SHE stands and tilts her dress.*) they are all looking up my dress.

WANDA. You'll get us arrested!

INEZ. By the police? They're looking, too! They're all looking up my dress, adoring me!! Tilt your skirt, Wanda, let them see your power.

WANDA. It's against the law —

INEZ. We're not exposing ourselves, Wanda. We've got dresses on. It's not our fault if they want to look.

WANDA. It's nasty.

INEZ. No, it's life!! It's eternity!

WANDA. It's ridiculous.

INEZ. Don't you want to feel good about yourself? Don't you want to feel like a worthy human being? Don't you want the power?

WANDA. I don't think of my na na as power.

INEZ. That's a big mistake, Wanda. It's the most powerful thing in the world. Come on, Wanda, let them see your power.

WANDA. I feel like a fool.

INEZ. You'll learn to love it. It's just the two of us, Wanda.

WANDA. (*Weakening.*) Inez —

INEZ. Step up, tilt your skirt. Try it, Wanda. Please, you won't regret it.

WANDA. Alright. (*Very gingerly does so.*)

INEZ. Just stand there. Think of all those men from all over. Close your eyes and see them. Men from all over America. There are Japanese, Chinese, Malaysians, Frenchmen, Englishmen, Irishmen, Germans, Poles, Russkies, Zimbabweans, Zanzabarians, maybe even Outer Mongolians. All these men of the world pass along the street, and Wanda, they're all looking. They're looking, and they see where they were created. They see and they long for the place they began. Feel their gaze.

WANDA. I do, and I'm not sure I like it.

INEZ. They're adoring us, Wanda. (*Her fervor is getting very high.*) Adoring us! We are the thing in which all humankind is created. We possess the cauldron. We are the survival of the species. We are the house of creation, the temple of God, the instrument of the goddess. We are all of that, Wanda. Feel them look, feel them adore, feel them desire. Take pity on them. Let their gaze penetrate your body.

WANDA. I'm feeling very warm, Inez.

INEZ. It's the power. The glory. Wars have been fought over us. All things that exist come from us. The power is surging. Let it fill your body. Feel it, Wanda. You are the power. They adore you. Say it, Wanda. Say, "I am the power." Come on, Wanda.

WANDA. I am the power.

INEZ. Humankind springs from me.

WANDA. Humankind springs from me.

INEZ. Creation occurs inside me.

WANDA. Creation occurs inside me.

INEZ. I am woman!! All powerful.

WANDA. I am all powerful woman. You're right, Inez. They are looking. I can feel it. They want me. They want me BAD. AND I LOVE IT. DID YOU HEAR ME, INEZ, I LOVE IT. LOVE, LOVE, LOVE IT. LOOK AT ME, ALL YOU PUNY LITTLE MEN. LOOK AT ME AND LOVE ME. SEE MY NA NA. SEE MY NA NA AND SHAKE WITH DESIRE. YES. YES. YES. YES.

INEZ. You don't want to overdo, Wanda.

WANDA. LOVE ME. LOVE ME. DO YOU HEAR ME?? LOVE ME. I AM THE POWER. I AM THE GLORY. FALL ON YOUR KNEES AND WORSHIP ME. I FEEL YOUR DESIRE RISING UPWARD. RISING UPWARD, AND I AM READY

FOR IT. I AM WANDA THE WONDERFUL!!

INEZ. (*Frightened.*) Wanda, the elevator's beginning to shake.

WANDA. CAN'T YOU FEEL IT, INEZ? CAN'T YOU FEEL THEIR DESIRE? FEEL IT PENETRATE!!!

INEZ. WANDA!! WANDA, YOU'VE GOT TO GET A HOLD OF YOURSELF!

WANDA. Oh, yes, yes, yes, yes, yes. YES, YES, YES, YES. OHHHHHHHHHHHHHHHHHH!

INEZ. Wanda!!

WANDA. What, Inez?

INEZ. Calm down! That's enough.

WANDA. Just a little more. I was really depressed.

INEZ. I know you were, but there's a limit to what they can take.

WANDA. Inez, I am the instrument of creation.

INEZ. That's what I've been trying to tell you.

WANDA. All power springs from me.

INEZ. Yes, and remember Wanda, whenever you get blue or down, you can always come here and take a ride in this glass elevator.

WANDA. It's better than any shrink, Inez!!

INEZ. And it won't go away for a long time. You're going to feel great for the next week or more.

WANDA. You think so?

INEZ. I know it. Every time I come up here and get recharged, men won't leave me alone for days.

WANDA. I'm ready.

INEZ. We'd better get going, Wanda.

WANDA. Inez, do you think we could do one more charge up as the elevator goes down?

INEZ. Couldn't do any harm, but don't get too carried away, Wanda.

WANDA. I won't. Inez, I want to thank you for this.

INEZ. Don't mention it, Wanda.

(THEY hold their dresses out as THEY descend and we hear the theme from Romeo and Juliet by Tschaikovsky at a point of high intensity.)

END OF PLAY

COSTUME

INEZ: A skirt coming to mid-calf, a relatively conservative blouse.

WANDA: A skirt coming to mid-calf, an even more conservative top.

SET

The set should consist of nothing more than tape placed on the stage floor to suggest the dimensions of the elevator.

JUST THINKING
by Alan Kravitz

Just Thinking was originally produced by Carousel Theatre Company, Inc., William-Kevin Young, Executive Director; Michael LaPolla, Artistic Director, as part of their one-act festival "A Circle of New Voices" at the The Studio in New York City on May 6, 1993. It was directed by Michael LaPolla and the cast was as follows:

JOSHUA...Evan Ferrante

THE PERFECT MAN....................James Patrick Stuart

THE NICE JEWISH GIRL...........................Danna Call

Stage Manager was Christine Weeks
Lighting Design by Denise Bourcier
Set Construction by Walter A. Ulasinski
Costumes by Danna Call
Sound by William-Kevin Young
Casting Director was Joan D'Incecco

Just Thinking was subsequently invited to the 18th Annual Off-Off-Broadway Short Play Festival, where it was presented under the same auspices, with the same director and cast.

CHARACTERS

JOSHUA HERSCHBERG — 12 years old, soon to be 13 and facing his bar mitzvah. He is also facing his feelings about his sexuality and this, for him, is confusing. He is not a nerd, but he is gawky, the kind of kid who accidentally steps to the left when he should be stepping to the right.

THE PERFECT MAN — A figment of Josh's imagination who comes to life. He is tall, very handsome and muscular. He is whatever Josh wants him to be.

THE NICE JEWISH GIRL — Also a figment of Josh's imagination, but shaped by the expectations of his family and not by his own desires. She is very pretty, but not drop-dead gorgeous. In the six years she has been planted in the back of Josh's mind, she has grown very fond of him. She is frustrated, though, because she doesn't seem to be able to get him.

TIME & PLACE

The present, on a weekday afternoon after Josh has returned home from junior high school.

Josh's bedroom.

JUST THINKING

SETTING: Joshua's bedroom. His bed is at center stage. There is a CD player on top of a dresser. On the opposite side of the room, there is a desk and chair. The room should also have a closet and a door. The room is decorated with movie memorabilia, including a miniature replica of an Oscar. Posters of pop culture stars hang on the wall.
AT RISE: JOSHUA walks toward center stage. One SPOTLIGHT follows him.
As JOSHUA walks, HE is reading a men's clothing catalogue, but as HE reaches center stage, HE stops reading the catalogue and looks toward the audience. His clothes are not trendy. HE wears a buttoned shirt and jeans.

JOSHUA. Orgasm ... ooooorgasm! God, what a wonderful word that is. In fact, of all the words in the English language, it's probably my favorite right now. You see, I'm twelve years old and I just took the comprehensive sex education course at Robert F. Kennedy Junior High. Jeez, since Miss Kleinbaum first said the word "orgasm" five weeks ago, I can't get it out of my mind. Which is not to say that the class was a total blast. Whoever thought sex could be so (*Grimaces.*) clinical? And of course we learned all this wonderful stuff about safe sex. Shit, I might have to spend my whole life wearing condoms on my thing every time I wanna do it. Yech! Very gross. But the class definitely had it's good points. It helped me a lot, I think. God, it seems everybody in school thinks about sex all the time. Well, in my case, not all the time. See, I'm gonna be thirteen in a couple of weeks and I'm also Jewish. That means my bar mitzvah gives sex a run for the money in the thought department. Sometimes I think the main purpose of a bar mitzvah now is to stop us Jewish kids from thinking about sex for a while. But it doesn't work. It just doesn't. I see some squirming out there each time I bring up the subject of sex. Some of you are probably uncomfortable with a twelve-year-old talking to you about such an "adult" subject. I can understand that, but when you think about it, there's probably no better person around to talk about sex. (*JOSHUA goes to his desk and picks up a test paper.*) You see, I just took my final exam in sex education two days ago. I got an "A" on it and I haven't had time to forget anything I had to remember for the test. (*HE swaggers confidently.*) So if any of you out there have forgotten what a vas deferens is and what it does, see me later. Of course, you could probably teach me a thing or two about sex, you being experienced at it and all. Well, at least most of you. I hope. Experience. That means you've had real orgasms, right? Orgasm. God, I can't say it enough. I just love the sound of the word. It starts out so strong — OR ... OR ... then it ends so light, like something floating on air (*Whispering.*) gasm. OR (*Whispering.*) gasm. Great combination. Great thing to have, too and between you and me, I've been having them as often as possible lately. (*JOSHUA turns to face the bedroom.*) And this is my room, where I've been having all my ORgasms. I guess I should tell you that I spend a lot of time alone in here. I live with my mother. She's a great mom and all that, but she still hasn't gotten over the death of my dad. He died when I was a baby. Had a heart attack at age thirty-two. Never sick a day in his life and then, bang! God, that sucks. But what can ya do, right? I spend lots of time in here after school. I study for my bar mitzvah in here. I want my family to be proud. But mostly I sit here and think about sex. Someone once said that the brain may be the worst thing God gives you because thinking too much can be very dangerous. I agree, but I think a lot anyway. I worry about that. If thinking too much is dangerous, can you imagine what thinking too much about sex leads to? Oy! (*JOSHUA plops down on the bed and starts looking through the catalogue.*) By the way, I'm reading this because Mom wants to buy me a new suit for my bar mitzvah party and she wants me to pick out something I like. Let's see. What's is the latest style for a young boy who, in one single morning, becomes a young man? (*JOSHUA sighs and starts flipping toward another section of the catalogue.*) Oh, who cares? Who really cares?

(THE PERFECT MAN steps out of the closet. HE is incredibly handsome, with chiseled cheekbones, dashing eyes and not a hair out of place. HE walks into the room like a model on a runway.)

PERFECT MAN. Excuse me, but don't you think all this might be easier for you if you would study the young boys' section of the catalogue?

JOSHUA. Wha ...

PERFECT MAN. Of course, I am pleased that you keep noticing me so much. I love the attention. *(HE extends his right hand for a shake.)* Hi, there!

JOSHUA. *(Alternating his eyes between the catalogue and THE PERFECT MAN.)* God, you're the ... the ...

PERFECT MAN. The man in the catalogue. The one you flip back to when you get frustrated. The one you've been thinking about since you got a load of *(HE starts posing like a model.)* page three.

JOSHUA. And page six and page nine and page eleven! *(HE checks the catalogue again.)* I, I can't believe this. Look! You're wearing the same outfit you're wearing on page eleven!

PERFECT MAN. That's right. That's the page you've been staring at the most.

JOSHUA. It's, it's very nice to meet you, sir, but why are you here?

PERFECT MAN. Please. There's no need to call me "sir." And I'm not really here. You see, I'm just a figment of your imagination. A very pleasing figment, mind you, but just a figment. Since I'm in your mind, I know what you're thinking. I know you're very nervous about your bar mitzvah. You don't want to embarrass your family.

JOSHUA. You know all that?

PERFECT MAN. Sure I do. I also know that you couldn't wait to get home from school today 'cause the air conditioning was on the fritz ...

JOSHUA. Could you believe that? How am I supposed to sit

though history class and learn about the Watergate scandal with shvitz pouring down my face?

PERFECT MAN. So you've come to your room and you've closed the door. And when you laid your eyes on me, you started to feel better. So, being the nice figment that I am, I thought I'd pop out and tell you everything's gonna be okay.

JOSHUA. Yeah? What's your name?

PERFECT MAN. Whatever you want it to be. It's up to you.

JOSHUA. What kind of job do you have?

PERFECT MAN. Whatever job you want me to have. Whatever you dream up, that's what I do. And I do it quite well, of course.

JOSHUA. Boy, this is great! Can you tell what I'm thinking now?

PERFECT MAN. Yes I can. You don't want me to be just a model, 'cause that's not a very ...

PERFECT MAN and JOSHUA. manly profession.

JOSHUA. Right!

PERFECT MAN. You're thinking that I'm a former No. 1 ranked tennis champ. I've won Wimbledon twice, the U.S. Open once ... and I really kicked ass at the French Open three years ago. You were right there in Paris to cheer me on.

JOSHUA. I was so proud of you.

PERFECT MAN. But you know I was feeling kind of empty that day. I was making millions, but people thought of me only as this drop-dead gorgeous jock! I wanted people to know that I was as smart as I was handsome and athletic. Smarter, even!

JOSHUA. So you went straight to Hollywood. At first, you thought of becoming an actor, but then you thought,"No. It's the director who's really in charge of a film." So you just marched yourself into the office of the biggest film company in Hollywood and told them you wanted to be a director. And just like that, you got your chance.

PERFECT MAN. And people think life is so hard ...

JOSHUA. But wait a minute! That film you directed was ... "Rain Man." Which became a huge hit and won four Academy Awards, including one for you as Best Director.

(JOSHUA runs toward his desk, picks up his miniature Oscar and hands it to THE PERFECT MAN.)

PERFECT MAN. That's right. Dusty thinks the world of my talents.

JOSHUA. The only thing is, I don't know what your next film's gonna be yet.

PERFECT MAN. Don't think about that too hard. The next time you read about a film that's getting rave reviews from everybody who's anybody, just start thinking I directed it.

JOSHUA. You're right! I'll do that. But for right now, I have to come up with a name for you.

(THE PREFECT MAN puts the Oscar down and stares at JOSHUA.)

PERFECT MAN. Kevin?

JOSHUA. Shit, you're good. Yeah, Kevin. You're Kevin. I always liked that name.

PERFECT MAN. Then that settles it. I'm Kevin.

JOSHUA. And your last name's ... (*Pause. HE looks over toward his CD collection.*) Simon. After Paul Simon.

(JOSHUA runs over to get a Simon and Garfunkel CD. HE shows it to THE PERFECT MAN.)

PERFECT MAN. Paul Simon. I know him personally.

JOSHUA. He wrote my favorite song of all time, "Bridge Over Troubled Water." I first heard it on an oldies station my mom listens to in the car. I always thought, "Who wants to listen to music from ancient times like the '70s?" But one day I heard that song and after that, I was spaced for days. God, could I relate to that song. When Garfunkel sings that song, it's like he's my friend, singing it just to me. (*HE starts singing, very off key.*)
When times get rough
And friends just can't be found
Like a ...

PERFECT MAN and JOSHUA. ... bridge over troubled water, I will lay me down.

(THEY smile at each other, then start laughing.)

PERFECT MAN. That's a great song to pick as your favorite.

JOSHUA. Thanks. I feel weird about leaving Garfunkel out of your name, but you just don't look like a Kevin Garfunkel. Kevin Simon just kinda flows better.

PERFECT MAN. I like Kevin Simon.

JOSHUA. *(Smiling.)* I'm glad. *(Nervous laugh.)* I like being with you.

(JOSHUA turns away from THE PERFECT MAN and puts back his CD.)

PERFECT MAN. Well, I certainly like being with you. I'd rather be with you than with anyone else.

JOSHUA. Really?

PERFECT MAN. Absolutely.

JOSHUA. You and me ... we're just so different, I mean, you being so successful and all.

PERFECT MAN. *(Sarcastic tone.)* Don't be ridiculous. Listen, the world may see me as handsome, smart, rich, a champion tennis star and a brilliant, Oscar-winning director with the world at my feet. And the world may see you as a scrawny kid who has few friends and locks himself in his room and fantasizes a lot, but hey, that's no big deal to me. I'll take you just as you are. You're the most important person in the world to me.

JOSHUA. Wow! That's ... that's the most meaningful thing anyone's said to me in a long time. I mean, my mother tells me she loves me all the time, but she says it so many times, it makes me sick.

PERFECT MAN. Your mom's reality. I'm fantasy. Don't forget that.

JOSHUA. I won't. But I wish I could have you with me all the time.

PERFECT MAN. You can! Just think of me, and I'll be right by you. I'm the most important person in the world to you right now and I know that.

(THE PERFECT MAN starts massaging Joshua's shoulders. JOSHUA relaxes.)

PERFECT MAN. Hey, you like that. Don't you?
JOSHUA. Yeah, I do. I think. *(JOSHUA pulls away.)*
PERFECT MAN. You can touch me, you know. You can reach out to me and touch me. That's what you want to do.

(JOSHUA walks toward THE PERFECT MAN and gently embraces him.)

PERFECT MAN. You want to lay your head in my arms so you can hear my heartbeat.
JOSHUA. Oh, yeah. It sounds great. *(HE smiles.)* Ba-bump. Ba-bump. Ba-bump.
PERFECT MAN. And you want me to hold you, just like this.
JOSHUA. Yes!
PERFECT MAN. Well, that's just what I'm here for. And I'm gonna keep doing it for as long as you want.
JOSHUA. God. Just like I've wanted for a long time.
PERFECT MAN. Well, you got me. Everything's gonna be okay, Josh. Everything's gonna be okay.
JOSHUA. Hmmmmm.

(SOUND: Fairy tale music.
This startles JOSHUA and THE PERFECT MAN and they cut off their embrace. THE NICE JEWISH GIRL merrily dances into the room. SHE is a pretty, statuesque woman. SHE is wearing a crown and a sequined hoop gown, both similar to what Billie Burke wore as Glinda in "The Wizard of Oz." SHE is holding a magic wand.)

NICE JEWISH GIRL. Ta da!

JOSHUA. Oh, my God!

NICE JEWISH GIRL. Joshua, my darling angel!

PERFECT MAN. Shit!

JOSHUA. It's ... it's you! The Nice Jewish Girl my family wants me to marry! You're here now, too?

NICE JEWISH GIRL. Yes, I am. It is my duty to be here. (*SHE looks toward THE PERFECT MAN.*) Hello, Kevin.

PERFECT MAN. Hi.

JOSHUA. You two know each other?

PERFECT MAN. We met while I was just a tiny figment swirling around in your head.

(THE PERFECT MAN holds JOSHUA in his arms.)

NICE JEWISH GIRL. Yes, we did. And you seem like such a pleasant fellow. So nice and handsome and talented. No wonder Dusty gushed about you at the Oscars. But you don't have to be here now. After all, (*THE NICE JEWISH GIRL pulls JOSHUA toward her chest.*) Josh can rest his head on MY chest. And feel MY heart. There, dear. Don't you feel wonderful now?

JOSHUA. Yeah. It feels nice to be with you. (*To THE PERFECT MAN.*) And you.

NICE JEWISH GIRL. My dear, this man is very busy out there in Hollywood and it's not nice to keep him away from his work, especially when I am available to please you on a split second's notice.

JOSHUA. But ... I'd like him to stay.

PERFECT MAN. And as long as he wants me to stay, I can stay. It's no problem.

JOSHUA. Great! You see that? It's no problem. (*HE looks at both of them.*) Then why does it feel like there's a problem?

NICE JEWISH GIRL. Well, Josh, cupcake, we must talk about what you're thinking about, being with this man and all.

JOSHUA. Why do we have to talk about it?

NICE JEWISH GIRL. Because thoughts like this simply must not continue. Oh darling, you're so young, so innocent, so impressionable. But don't you realize, if you keep thinking like this, you're going to be a (*Snarling, monster voice.*) HOMOSEXUAL? You don't want to be a (*Snarling, monster voice.*) HOMOSEXUAL, do you?

JOSHUA. No, I don't. (*To THE PERFECT MAN.*) I just wanted to hang out with you. That's all.

(*THE PERFECT MAN gets up off the bed and confronts THE NICE JEWISH GIRL.*)

PERFECT MAN. Wait a minute, what is this? Who do you think you are? Josh and I were having a perfectly nice time, then you just pop in and ruin it.

NICE JEWISH GIRL. Well, excuse me for barging in, but Josh would be much better off if he thought about me. And he does think about me quite often. Don't you, Josh? (*THE NICE JEWISH GIRL caresses JOSHUA and runs her fingers through his hair.*)

JOSHUA. Um hm.

NICE JEWISH GIRL. Oh, I just loooove your hair. It's so soft and wavy. I think it's one of your best features.

JOSHUA. I think it's my only good feature.

PERFECT MAN. And I think all of this sucks. Josh thinks of you only because his family tells him to think of you. (*HE turns to JOSHUA, flexes his muscles and strikes a suggestive pose.*) But he thinks of me because I'm the one he really wants.

NICE JEWISH GIRL. Ha!

JOSHUA. Nice. Very nice.

NICE JEWISH GIRL. Josh, stop thinking like that!

PERFECT MAN. (*To NICE JEWISH GIRL.*) And I'm sure you realize he has an erection right now, just as he had before we were so rudely interrupted.

(*JOSHUA goes to his desk and quickly sits down in his chair, embarrassed.*)

NICE JEWISH GIRL. Josh, pumpkin, do you realize what life would be like for you as a (*Snarly, monster voice.*) FAYGALEH? Your family would just plotz if they found out. Your poor dear mother would have a heart attack, just like your father did. Would you want that, young man?

JOSHUA. No. Of course not.

NICE JEWISH GIRL. And then there's the rest of the world. I mean, the way they treat those people, who in their right minds would want to be a homosexual?

PERFECT MAN. Fuck this. I've heard enough.

NICE JEWISH GIRL. A fantasy figure who swears. How uncouth.

PERFECT MAN. You don't understand anything. I'm the one Josh wants. Not you.

NICE JEWISH GIRL. You? You're a man.

PERFECT MAN. So what?

NICE JEWISH GIRL. So what? My goodness, the fact that you're a man makes all the difference in the world. Joshua, may I please have some time alone with you to talk? Besides, I'm sure this man has another movie to direct and an Oscar to win.

PERFECT MAN. According to Josh, here, yes I do. But that can wait. (*HE looks toward JOSHUA.*) I'm gonna fight for this little guy. His feelings for me are natural.

NICE JEWISH GIRL. His feelings for you are very harmful. And I'm here to change that.

JOSHUA. Excuse me. Could I say something?

NICE JEWISH GIRL. Not now, dear. We're deciding your sexuality.

(*THE PERFECT MAN pushes THE NICE JEWISH GIRL aside, goes over to JOSHUA and rubs his shoulders.*)

PERFECT MAN. There's not much to decide. Josh is gonna be in my arms, not your's.

NICE JEWISH GIRL. And what makes you so sure of that?

PERFECT MAN. There's a simple answer. (*Suggestively.*) I can make him very happy

NICE JEWISH GIRL. Stop that! I know Josh is not ... one of those.

PERFECT MAN. How do you know that?

NICE JEWISH GIRL. Well, he likes to watch football.

(JOSHUA shakes his head, smiling.)

PERFECT MAN. Ah yes, he loves the sight of those sweaty, gargantuan men huddling up together and patting each other on the tush.

(JOSHUA pouts.)

PERFECT MAN. It's his favorite team sport.
NICE JEWISH GIRL. Josh likes to watch baseball.

(JOSHUA shakes his head and smiles.)

PERFECT MAN. Sure he does, especially when Mr. Jockey briefs, Jim Palmer's one of the announcers.

(JOSHUA pouts.)

NICE JEWISH GIRL. Well, Josh is very devoted to his family.

(JOSHUA shakes his head and smiles.)

NICE JEWISH GIRL. He dreams of having one of his own some day. He loves looking through family photo albums.
PERFECT MAN. With special attention paid to every photo of his Cousin Rob, the surfer from San Diego.

(JOSHUA pouts.)

NICE JEWISH GIRL. You've got Josh all wrong.

(JOSHUA shakes his head and smiles.)

NICE JEWISH GIRL. Why, he watches football purely for the fun and excitement of the game. And he watches Jim Palmer because he wants to be informed about baseball. And he cherishes those photos of Cousin Rob because, with Rob being far away on the other side of the country, Josh doesn't get to see him much. Oh, he's such a sweet, devoted boy. (*SHE runs her fingers through JOSHUA's hair.*) And a boy with beautiful hair, too. Ooo, I can't get enough of it.

PERFECT MAN. I don't know. He's thinking pret-ty heavily about me.

NICE JEWISH GIRL. He won't be for long. Josh?

JOSHUA. Yes?

NICE JEWISH GIRL. I must tell you something.

(THE NICE JEWISH GIRL and JOSHUA walk toward the bed. THE NICE JEWISH GIRL sits at the edge of the bed, while JOSHUA stands in front of her.)

NICE JEWISH GIRL. Remember the other day, when mother sat you down and showed you her most prized possession?

JOSHUA. Her wedding ring?

NICE JEWISH GIRL. Yes. And she told you that on your wedding day, she'd give it to you to give to your bride, and you thought of me and I got to take a look. And seeing that ring sent shivers down my spine. (*Sweet, but sarcastic tone.*) That little diamond, with just a tiny little gleam left, it was so beautiful.

JOSHUA. Mom said Dad couldn't afford a bigger diamond. It didn't matter to her, though.

NICE JEWISH GIRL. And it won't matter to me, either. I can't wait to have that little ring on my finger. I can see it now. Your mother will be crying with joy. Your family will be all smiles, including Cousin Rob — and his charming wife who you'll just love so much. You and me, we'll be under that chuppa and we'll be more in love than any two people in the world!

JOSHUA. We sure will. It'll be great!

NICE JEWISH GIRL. I love you, Joshua.

JOSHUA. I love you too, Nice Jewish Girl.

(THEY hug.)

PERFECT MAN. Aw, this is so sweet. Too bad I don't believe a word of it. (*Suggestively to THE NICE JEWISH GIRL.*) You may be Josh's bride, but I'm his best man.

NICE JEWISH GIRL. How can you say that?

PERFECT MAN. Because Josh is gay.

JOSHUA. (*Turns toward THE PERFECT MAN.*) I'm not a fag!

PERFECT MAN. Josh!

JOSHUA. I'm not one of those people. I just like being with you. That's all.

PERFECT MAN. Josh, I understand where you're coming from, but there are things you haven't quite figured out yet.

NICE JEWISH GIRL. No, no. I'm afraid there are things you haven't figured out. This innocent young man is not gay and he never will be. Josh is attracted to women. (*THE NICE JEWISH GIRL puts her arm around JOSHUA.*) He's just a little shy, that's all. A little awkward. It's just a crazy phase he's going through.

PERFECT MAN. Yeah, right.

NICE JEWISH GIRL. And I'm gonna change that all right now.

PERFECT MAN. And how do you expect to do that?

NICE JEWISH GIRL. By just being myself. I can charm any man alive.

PERFECT MAN. In that gown?

NICE JEWISH GIRL. A man from the movies should realize that this is a close replica of the gown worn by Glinda, the good witch, in "The Wizard of Oz."

JOSHUA. That's my favorite movie character of all time. And "The Wizard of Oz" is my favorite movie of all time! I have it on tape. I can watch it over and over again.

PERFECT MAN. An insatiable fascination with "The Wizard of Oz?" Now, if that ain't a gay in training, I don't know what is.

NICE JEWISH GIRL. (*Getting angry.*) You're crazy! Joshua always has me dress this way. He's imagined me with many of Glinda's qualities. I stand for nothing but pure goodness. I have loads of charm and I'm adored by all. And as anyone can plainly see, I'm not only beautiful, I'm ravishing! And I have brains to match.

JOSHUA. Yeah. She's a nuclear physicist.

PERFECT MAN. A nuclear physicist who dresses like Glinda. Oprah would have a field day with this broad.

NICE JEWISH GIRL. And that's not all. I come from a very wealthy family. With me, Joshua would want for nothing. And I'll continue right on with my work after I give birth to Josh's three perfect children. With me, Josh will have beauty, brilliance and big bucks. What else could any mortal male want?

JOSHUA. It's a great deal. I would have a great life.

NICE JEWISH GIRL. I would make sure of that, darling. (*THE NICE JEWISH GIRL winks at JOSHUA.*)

PERFECT MAN. Well! I must say the heat you're generating is intoxicating. I must make myself more comfortable.

(THE PERFECT MAN takes off his shirt. JOSHUA stares intently at his chest.)

JOSHUA. Holy shit!

NICE JEWISH GIRL. What are you doing? Put that back on!

PERFECT MAN. Why should I? If your charisma really works for Josh, it should be able to withstand some minor distractions.

JOSHUA. Holy shit!

NICE JEWISH GIRL. Well, two can play this game, big boy! (*SHE grabs JOSHUA.*) I'm gonna make you learn more about your favorite word.

(JOSHUA throws THE NICE JEWISH GIRL off of him and jumps out of bed.)

JOSHUA. Hoooly shit!

PERFECT MAN. Right now, I think those are his favorite words.

JOSHUA. (*Runs toward the door.*) Oh, God, I can't stand this anymore.

NICE JEWISH GIRL. Where are you going?

JOSHUA. The bathroom.

PERFECT MAN. Hey, pal. Aren't you forgetting something?

(THE PERFECT MAN tosses JOSHUA the catalogue. JOSHUA catches it.)

JOSHUA. Oh, yeah! Thanks. See ya! *(JOSHUA runs out of the room and closes the door.)*
NICE JEWISH GIRL. Joshua, wait! Don't you want a picture of me? A bathing suit shot *Sports Illustrated* would kill for! *(SHE tries to open the door, but it will not open.)* Damn it, open this door!

(THE PERFECT MAN lies confidently on the bed and laughs.)

NICE JEWISH GIRL. Oh, shut up. I can't believe the problems you cause.
JOSHUA. Oooh, oooh ...
PERFECT MAN. Problems? I do believe Josh is quite content right now.
NICE JEWISH GIRL. I don't think so.

(THE NICE JEWISH GIRL takes out her magic wand and spits on her hands.)

NICE JEWISH GIRL. Watch and weep. *(SHE waves the wand three times at the door.)* He dreams of me, but he doesn't give me any powers. Shit. Open this door!
JOSHUA. Ooooh .... aaaah.
PERFECT MAN. *(Looks at his watch.)* Too late! Game, set and match. Oy, not even five minutes. These kids are amazing these days.
NICE JEWISH GIRL. *(Paces the room, then sits down.)* Great. Just great. Shit, this isn't supposed to happen. Fantasies are supposed to be happy, right? Everything is wonderful. What dreams are made of, right?

(The door opens. JOSHUA walks out, headed back toward the bed.

*JOSHUA plops back down on the bed. THE PERFECT MAN is
near him.)*

JOSHUA. Thanks.
PERFECT MAN. You're welcome.
NICE JEWISH GIRL. Well. Isn't this a pair? Prince Charming
and Charlie Brown basking in afterglow.
JOSHUA. You're angry at me. Why do you have to be angry at
me?
NICE JEWISH GIRL. I'll tell you why I'm angry at you.

(SHE stands up. THE PERFECT MAN puts on his shirt.)

NICE JEWISH GIRL. For six years, I've been in your mind —
ever since Aunt Sylvia bitched and bitched that your cousin Mike
was marrying a shiksa, like flags would have to fly at half staff if
some goysha blood came into the family. She turned to you and
said, (*Mimicking an old lady's voice.*) "Joshua, Aunt Sylvia's not
coming to your wedding if you don't marry a nice Jewish girl."
(*Mimics a drag on a cigarette. To PERFECT MAN.*) Well, Aunt
Sylvia is like God to him. (*THE NICE JEWISH GIRL sits down on
the bed with JOSHUA and THE PERFECT MAN.*) He couldn't
bear the thought of her not being at his wedding. So he started
thinking what a nice Jewish girl would be like. And I was born.
(*To JOSHUA.*) And in these years, I've gotten to know you. To
love you. To become a part of you. But for the past couple of
years, dear, it's been rough, 'cause I've had to share space in your
mind with these guys. I keep trying to forget they're there. I keep
telling myself they're gonna go away, but they never do. And after
six years of doing nothing but trying to please you, what happens?
The hunk from hell comes along, and I'm chopped liver! (*THE
NICE JEWISH GIRL gets up and stands toward center stage.*)
PERFECT MAN. I'm sorry. I'm truly sorry. And since Josh is a
little confused right now, I'll say that for the both of us. This was
just one of those things. You shouldn't be angry at Josh. Things are
happening to him that he just couldn't control. And I got caught up
in this and — bang.

NICE JEWISH GIRL. I'll say.

PERFECT MAN. I never meant to hurt you. I'm truly sorry.

NICE JEWISH GIRL. Joshua, this isn't going to work. You're gonna be hard to say good-bye to.

JOSHUA. (*Stands and goes toward THE NICE JEWISH GIRL.*) No! We can't say good-bye. You're gonna stay with me.

NICE JEWISH GIRL. But you're gonna be miserable.

JOSHUA. But I'm not gonna keep doing this. I'm not a fairy.

PERFECT MAN. The word is "gay," Josh.

JOSHUA. Well, according to everyone at school, the word is "fairy." They call me that all the time and I hate it. (*To NICE JEWISH GIRL.*) But you and me, we're gonna work at making life better. I mean, I was just having fun here. This isn't the way I'm gonna be forever. I'm gonna do it with girls. I really am.

NICE JEWISH GIRL. You are, huh?

JOSHUA. Of course I am. You just have to be patient.

NICE JEWISH GIRL. My picture should be next to the word "patient" in the dictionary. For six years, you make me wear this jeweled contraption. I'll bet Billie Burke got out of this thing the second the director yelled "cut." But I have to wear this all the time, 'cause it pleases you. And now, you don't even want me.

JOSHUA. That dress looks beautiful on you. That's why I want you to wear it. And I do want you. I'd be crazy if I didn't want you.

NICE JEWISH GIRL. I just don't think there's a chance for us.

(JOSHUA walks toward his desk and sits down. THE NICE JEWISH GIRL follows him.)

NICE JEWISH GIRL. I'm very fond of you, Josh, but I'm sure there are lots of nice Jewish boys who'd love to fantasize about me. All it takes is one sharp infliction of guilt by a domineering relative and presto! I'll be reborn.

JOSHUA. You didn't listen to me. I said I wasn't gonna think about men anymore, and I'm not. When I ... do it, ya know? I'll only think about you. I promise.

NICE JEWISH GIRL. (*With a faint smile.*) So you'll be

thinking of me at least three times a day, huh?

JOSHUA. And on days when I'm really bored, four, five and six times.

NICE JEWISH GIRL. Wow! Warren Beatty Jr. This is hard to resist. (*SHE sighs.*) I'm not sure about this. Can you to prove to me that you could be attracted to me?

JOSHUA. Sure. How?

NICE JEWISH GIRL. By doing it and thinking only of me. It would be good practice for you.

(THE NICE JEWISH GIRL pulls JOSHUA toward the bathroom, but JOSHUA pulls away.)

JOSHUA. I can't yet. I just did it a few minutes ago. Even Warren Beatty Jr. needs a break.

(THE NICE JEWISH GIRL gently pushes JOSHUA toward the bed. JOSHUA sits down on the bed.)

NICE JEWISH GIRL. Then how 'bout a kiss? A nice, sweet, soft, sensual kiss. Is that too much to ask for?

PERFECT MAN. Wait a minute!

JOSHUA. (*Gets up off the bed and goes to his desk and chair.*) God! If I have to face this shit every time I'm in the mood, my orgasms better start lasting a lot longer.

PERFECT MAN. Josh, listen to me. You've got to learn that the experience we shared together wasn't wrong, even if everybody thinks it is.

JOSHUA. Well, it was wrong.

NICE JEWISH GIRL. (*Lifting her head up.*) Amen!

JOSHUA. I'm ashamed of what I did with you. I don't wanna ever think about you again.

PERFECT MAN. You can't be serious.

JOSHUA. I sure am serious. You came here to please me. Well, I'm not pleased. I'm very confused. The guys at school, they don't have fantasies about other guys. They have fantasies about girls. And that's what I'm gonna have.

PERFECT MAN. Josh, if you just listen to me, you'd realize how unfair you're being to yourself ...

JOSHUA. (*Starts yelling.*) Stop that! Just stop that! I'm not a fag! I'm not a fucking fag!

(*JOSHUA sits down at his desk. THE PERFECT MAN goes to comfort JOSHUA, but the THE NICE JEWISH GIRL pushes him out of the way and gets to JOSHUA first.*)

NICE JEWISH GIRL. It's all right, dear. It's all right. Just let it out. I'm here. I'll always be here. (*Turning to THE PERFECT MAN.*) Now, do you see what you've done? Do you see?

(*THE PERFECT MAN shakes his head in a daze.*)

NICE JEWISH GIRL. Why don't you just get the hell out of here?

JOSHUA. Yeah! Go back in the closet!

PERFECT MAN. Only you can make me go back in the closet, pal.

(*JOSHUA looks toward THE PERFECT MAN.*)

PERFECT MAN. And it looks like you're gonna make me do that. (*HE stops and turns to look at JOSHUA.*) But I gotta tell you, you're not gonna be able to get rid of me. No matter how hard you try, you'll never get rid of me.

JOSHUA. You're crazy! (*JOSHUA gets up and walks toward his CD collection.*)

PERFECT MAN. I know this isn't easy for you. With her, you'll never have to worry about what people might think if you two took a walk in the park and you were so into each other that you want to put your arms around each other. And when you're at work, you'll be able to call home and say, "Honey, what's for dinner?" without the whole office wondering about you. Yeah, life'll be easier. But it won't be better.

NICE JEWISH GIRL. Will you just shut up and go away!

PERFECT MAN. Well, it seems like Josh has a hard time getting me to go away. Don't you, pal?

JOSHUA. No, I don't.

PERFECT MAN. Then how come I'm still here? You must want me if you can't get me out of your mind.

JOSHUA. I'm not a fairy! That's the last fucking time I'm going to tell you that! Get outta here! Now!

THE PERFECT MAN. The two of us, we can make magic, Josh. Real magic! But I can't make you see that, and that frustrates the hell out of me. Good-bye, Josh. I hope you find the happiness you're looking for. (*THE PERFECT MAN turns toward the closet.*)

JOSHUA. Good-bye. I'm sorry I yelled at you.

PERFECT MAN. It's okay. (*THE PERFECT MAN turns back toward JOSHUA.*)

JOSHUA. I, I hope you find the happiness you're looking for, too.

PERFECT MAN. I still think there's a chance for us ... Oh, forget it. I give up. (*HE walks back toward the closet door.*) Hey, Josh?

JOSHUA. What?

PERFECT MAN. Before I go, can you look me in the eyes? Please. Can you do that?

JOSHUA. Yes.

(*JOSHUA and THE PERFECT MAN look into each other's eyes.*)

PERFECT MAN. Good.

(*THE PERFECT MAN closes the closet door. JOSHUA looks at the closed door as if HE is lost.*)

JOSHUA. Well.

NICE JEWISH GIRL. Well.

JOSHUA. Well, there. He's gone.

NICE JEWISH GIRL. He sure is.

JOSHUA. You wanna just talk or something?

NICE JEWISH GIRL. You know what I wanna do.

JOSHUA. Yeah. But we can't do it yet. I'm ... I'm just not ready.

NICE JEWISH GIRL. Well, I can certainly change that.

(THE NICE JEWISH GIRL sits down on the edge of the bed. JOSHUA faces her. JOSHUA hesitates, then kisses THE NICE JEWISH GIRL.)

JOSHUA. Am I good at this? Am I really good?

NICE JEWISH GIRL. You sure are, you sweet thing!

(THE NICE JEWISH GIRL kisses JOSHUA all over his face.)

JOSHUA. God, this is better than Disney World.

NICE JEWISH GIRL. Oh, God! *(THE NICE JEWISH GIRL gets up.)*

JOSHUA. What?

NICE JEWISH GIRL. You thought of him!

JOSHUA. Only for a second.

NICE JEWISH GIRL. It would have been longer if I hadn't pulled away.

JOSHUA. I don't know what came over me.

NICE JEWISH GIRL. Oh, pu-lease!

JOSHUA. Look, I know you think I'm not interested in girls, but you're wrong. *(HE reaches under his bed.)* See this? The *Playboy* Jimmy Goldfarb stole from his father's closet. I haven't looked at it yet, but boy, I've wanted to and I think I will right now. Oh, jeez, just get a load of the playmate of the month, Amber McKnight! Let's see what it says about this girl. She's a model and she wants to be an actress and she's real determined to reach her goal 'cause whenever she sees something she wants, she goes for it.

NICE JEWISH GIRL. Josh?

JOSHUA. Uh huh?

NICE JEWISH GIRL. When you see a centerfold and the first thing you go for is the article ... it's not a good sign.

(THEY stare into each other's eyes. JOSHUA puts the magazine away. HE sits down at his desk and buries his head in his hands. THE NICE JEWISH GIRL puts her arms around him.)

JOSHUA. I am one of those fairies, aren't I? I am one of those fags ...

NICE JEWISH GIRL. Gays, Joshua. Gays. Look, can I tell you something? You're not the first kid to be confused like this. Give yourself a break. You have your whole life to figure this out. Save some of those brain cells for other things. Like algebra.

JOSHUA. Oh, God. I'm alone. I'm so alone.

NICE JEWISH GIRL. No, you're not. That's not true.

JOSHUA. Yes, it is. I mean, nobody I know is gay. No one at school is gay. No one in my family is gay. No one famous is gay, either.

NICE JEWISH GIRL. There's a lot of famous gays. Only they don't say they're gay, so you don't know they exist. Look, I may not be gay, but I know what it's like to feel different. I mean, if you think it's easy for a nuclear physicist to dress like this, you've got another thing coming. Look, you have to go with your feelings. And you mustn't let anyone push you around. And I'm telling you this because, God knows, people are gonna try to push you around. *(Pause.)* God knows, I tried.

JOSHUA. I don't even know what men ... do, ya know? That's the one thing Miss Kleinbaum couldn't teach us about. She just skimmed over the entire subject of homosexuality. She just said sometimes men love men and women love women, but she didn't say anymore, except that these things don't normally happen. Maybe she was embarrassed. It was so weird, 'cause she was so open about everything else.

(THE PERFECT MAN again steps out of the closet.)

PERFECT MAN. If you ask me, one of those stupid parents groups probably got to her.

JOSHUA. I thought I asked you to leave.

PERFECT MAN. How can I? You think of me when you kiss

her. You think of me when you read *Playboy*. I'm not getting a minute to myself here. I'm not even getting a chance to consider scripts.

JOSHUA. That's okay. You're directing Kevin Costner's new movie. I just decided.

PERFECT MAN. Thanks. I'll make sure you're on the set when we film the skinny dipping scene.

JOSHUA. Well, as long as you're back, can you tell me what men (*Pause.*) do, ya know?

PERFECT MAN. Well, I don't actually know. If you'd let me attend more Hollywood parties, I'll find out for you. (*THE PERFECT MAN sits on the bed, next to THE NICE JEWISH GIRL.*)

JOSHUA. (*To NICE JEWISH GIRL.*) I guess you don't know, either, right?

NICE JEWISH GIRL. 'Fraid not, angel. Although I always thought that some of those male munchkins cackled just a little too merrily amongst themselves.

(*THE NICE JEWISH GIRL and THE PERFECT MAN giggle like munchkins. THEY playfully slap each other and push each other.*)

JOSHUA. Guys!

(*THE NICE JEWISH GIRL and THE PERFECT MAN immediately stop and turn their attention to JOSHUA.*)

JOSHUA. So how am I going to find out?

PERFECT MAN. The same way you find out about everything else. You ask.

JOSHUA. I can't ask my mom. That's for sure. She blushes when I talk about normal sex. I can't imagine talking to her about fag sex.

(*THE PERFECT MAN coughs.*)

JOSHUA. Sorry. Gay sex. *(Pause.)* Hey, Glinda?

NICE JEWISH GIRL. *(Slightly exasperated.)* Yes, angel?

JOSHUA. Don't be mad at me. If you want me to, I could mention you to Jimmy Goldfarb. I'm sure he has no idea what Amber wants to do with her life.

NICE JEWISH GIRL. That would be very sweet of you, but I think I'm still going to pop up in your thoughts every now and then. If nothing else, we'll still be friends.

JOSHUA. That's great! I'd like that! But what if there might come a time when I would like us to be, you know, more than friends?

NICE JEWISH GIRL. Well, I guess if that's what you'd want, then we'd be more than friends.

(THE PERFECT MAN coughs, then puts his arms around JOSHUA.)

NICE JEWISH GIRL. But I have a feeling I won't be washing your underwear anytime soon.

PERFECT MAN. *(Looks at his watch.)* Hey, I smell pot roast! Time for dinner!

NICE JEWISH GIRL. I am famished myself. Why don't we all go down to eat?

JOSHUA. Sure. You guys go wash up. I'll be down in a minute.

PERFECT MAN. Make it quick, huh? We're fantasies. We can't eat without you.

(THE PERFECT MAN and THE NICE JEWISH GIRL start walking out the door.)

NICE JEWISH GIRL. That's okay. It'll give us a chance to chat. I've known Josh longer than you have. Now, when he hides his broccoli in his napkin, give him a nudge ...

(THE PERFECT MAN and THE NICE JEWISH GIRL leave the room.)

JOSHUA. (*To the audience.*) You guys gotta promise me something. You can't tell my mother that I might be a fag.

PERFECT MAN (*Offstage.*) Josh!

JOSHUA. Sorry. That I might be gay. It'll kill her. She's always telling me that I should go to college, get married, get a nice-paying job and move out of the house. That always makes her smile. Especially when she gets to the moving out of the house part. I don't wanna hurt her. And please don't tell anyone else I know, either. Not a soul, okay? If they know, then no one'll wanna come to my bar mitzvah party. Imagine, all this trouble, all because I like one man. (*Pause. JOSHUA looks at the catalogue and sits down on the bed.*) Maybe I'll stay after school tomorrow. Talk to Miss Kleinbaum. Yeah. That's what I'll do. She might freak out, but she still talks to Todd Burger, and he's the one who tried to replace our sex ed film with a Penthouse video. If she can handle that, she can handle me. But when I talk to her, I'm gonna ask her why she didn't teach about me in her class. Because I deserve answers. I deserve to be included. (*Pause.*) I deserve to eat. All this thinking's making me hungry. (*JOSHUA heads toward the door.*) Well, I gotta go. I'd invite you to come eat with us, but I don't think there's enough pot roast. Broccoli for days, but not enough pot roast. Anyway, take care, now. And remember. You promised. (*JOSHUA leaves the room and slams the door.*)

CURTAIN

Alan Kravitz

Alan Kravitz is an award-winning journalist and playwright. His full-length plays include *Back Seat Drivers* and *Sledding Down Nicholson.*

PASQUINI THE MAGNIFICENT

by Sam Ingraffia

*To my wife, Maggie,
for laughing at my jokes . . .
and believing.*

Pasquini The Magnificent was first presented as a project at The Company of Angels Theatre, in Hollywood, California. It was directed by Michael Haney and had the following cast:

JACK THOMAS.................................Don Oscar Smith

ENZO PASQUINI.....................................Paul Michael

MARION KELLY ....Toni Sawyer

Pasquini The Magnificent was presented at the Eighteenth Annual Off-Off Broadway Play Festival by Theatre 40. It was directed by Ricardo Gutierrez and had the following cast (in order of appearance):

JACK THOMAS ....Jerry Beal

ENZO PASQUINI ....Milt Kogan

MARION KELLY...................................Rachel Davies

The author wishes to thank Christopher Michael Moore and Stewart J. Zully, the producers of Theatre 40's Fourth Annual One-Act Festival; and also Andre Barron, James Bartz, William Blair, Jody Price, Barbara Sammeth, Gloria Stroock, Jan O'Connor, Michael Haney, Ricardo Gutierrez and both casts, for working so hard to make the play a success in Los Angeles and New York.

And special thanks to The Golden West Playwrights for their help and support in developing the play.

CHARACTERS

JACK THOMAS – 40's, a wholesale meat broker

ENZO PASQUINI – 50's, an aging magician

MARION KELLY – 40's, an attractive housewife

TIME & PLACE

The back room of a restaurant.

The time is the present.

PASQUINI THE MAGNIFICENT

SETTING: A small storage room. A few folding chairs and a card table are the only furniture. There are shelves on all of the walls, except for one that is covered with beat up lockers. On one of the shelves is a portable tape player. Restaurant supplies are stacked all around the room. There is a small mirror on the wall, with a sign next to it that reads, "Lavas Las Manos" [Wash Your Hands]. There are three doors in the room; one has "Employee Restroom" written across it, the other is slightly ajar and opens onto a hallway, the third has a sign on it that reads, "Emergency Exit."

The present. 8:15 p.m.

AT RISE: RAIN and THUNDER can be faintly heard, mingled with an offstage voice.

JACK. (*O.S.*) This is the lounge for the employees.

(The door to the hall opens and JACK THOMAS, a man in his 40's, with a ferret-like face, dressed in a tuxedo, leads ENZO PASQUINI into the storage room. ENZO closes his umbrella and shakes it.

ENZO is a bulky man in his 50's, dressed in an overcoat. HE limps slightly on his left side as HE walks.

HE is carrying a large leather suitcase and a garment bag. His coat is wet from the rain. Across the suitcase, in large, white, block letters, is stenciled, "Pasquini The Magnificent."

THEY both look around the room.

ENZO sets down the case and the garment bag and checks the lockers. They are all locked.

JACK. I'm sure we can get somebody to open one of those for you.

ENZO. That'd be good. (*ENZO continues to look around the*

room.) My agent got you the tapes?
JACK. Yep. All set. Two back here and one for your show.

(There is an awkward silence.)

JACK. Let me take your umbrella. (*JACK takes the umbrella, opens the fire exit door and begins to shake it out.*) So, Rex thinks this young Japanese comic is a hot ticket. I told him it was a mistake. Would he listen? No. He thinks he knows show business because his stupid brother-in-law used to be on a soap opera twenty years ago.

(ENZO nods, only half paying attention, as HE continues to study the room.)

ENZO. Does the bathroom work?
JACK. Uh ... I couldn't say for sure. Probably.

(ENZO opens the door and walks into the bathroom.)

JACK. (*A little louder, so that Enzo can hear him.*) So ... The kid gets a job in Vegas and we're history. Then, as if that wasn't bad enough, Rex gets the chicken pox. What kind of a disease is that for a grown man to get? I had it when I was nine years old. My brother Larry and I both got it at the same time, right in the middle of the summer. (*JACK wanders into the bathroom, singing a popular melody.*)
ENZO. (*O.S.*) Hey !
JACK. (*O.S.*) Sorry! (*JACK hurries out of the bathroom and begins to adjust his tie in the mirror.*) Uh, anyway, the committee asks me to jump in, being as I am a former entertainment chairman. Well, I was more than happy to jump in. And I'd just like to take this moment to say, that I feel extremely fortunate, that a performer of your caliber was available. This never happened when I was head of the —
ENZO. (*Walking out of bathroom.*) It works.
JACK. Great.

(ENZO hangs up the garment bag, then places his suitcase on the table.)

JACK. You know, you may not be aware of this but we have quite a tradition for top notch entertainment at our dinners. Three years ago I booked Shelly Berman. I tell ya, I laughed so hard, I thought I was gonna pee my pants. The year before that ... *Sandy Baron.* And now ... Pasquini The Magnificent. Yes, sir, The Wholesale Meat Distributor's Annual Dinner has quite a rich tradition.

ENZO. When do you think I'll be going on?

JACK. Oh ... About forty minutes.

(ENZO checks his watch.)

JACK. They're still eating right now. Don't wanna rush 'em.

(ENZO nods and unbuttons his overcoat. HE is wearing tuxedo pants and a white tee shirt. HE starts to hang his coat.)

JACK. *(Smiling)* I bet you can't guess what the main course is?

ENZO. What?

JACK. I said, I bet you can't guess what the main course is?

ENZO. I have no idea.

JACK. That was a joke. We're all wholesale meat distributors. The main course is steak.

ENZO. *(Trying to be pleasant.)* That makes sense.

(There is another awkward silence.)

JACK. So, I guess you're all set?

ENZO. Looks like. *(ENZO is waiting for Jack to leave.)*

JACK. Once again, I'd like to apologize for the fact that we have to get you your money next week.

ENZO. It's okay.

JACK. I explained to your agent that Rex gave a substantial

guarantee to the comedian. As soon as —

ENZO. I said, it's okay.

JACK. Great. And I will certainly be more than happy to comp your agent.

ENZO. Uh ... If that's a problem, you —

JACK. No problem at all.

ENZO. I mean, he's seen my act a thousand times.

JACK. Please. It's the least I can do.

ENZO. Okay.

(The MEN look at each other. After a beat, JACK pulls a piece of paper out of his pocket.)

JACK. Maybe we should discuss your introduction before I go? I have some notes your agent, Mr. Rosenfeld, gave me.

(ENZO sighs and tries to be polite.)

JACK. *(Reading.)* Atlantic City, Las Vegas ... Ed Sullivan — You know ... I remember seeing you on Ed Sullivan. You were great! What was your famous trick?

ENZO. Pandora's Box.

JACK. Pandora's Box! You stuck swords through a person in the box!

ENZO. *(Snapping.)* No!

(There is an awkward moment.)

ENZO. *(With a forced smile.)* Uh ... Pandora's Box was ... Someone from the audience would come up. I'd hand them an empty box. Without me ever touching it ... I'd make things appear in it, like their watch, or their wallet.

JACK. *(Disappointed.)* Really? *(Pause.)* Well, I'm sure it was great. *(Beat.)* Ed Sullivan's kind of an old credit, anyway. Maybe I won't even mention that one. *(Reading again.)* Steve Allen, The Smothers Brothers ... Uh ... Any recent television credits?

ENZO. *(Curt.)* No.

JACK. (*Trying to lighten the moment.*) Maybe I'll just say numerous television appearances and highlight Atlantic City and Las Vegas?

ENZO. Fine.

JACK. (*Giving Enzo a conspiratorial wink.*) You know, we have something in common. I used to dabble in the magic arts a little myself.

ENZO. (*Trying to be civil.*) Really?

JACK. Never with the expertise of a Pasquini The Magnificent. (*A nasty laugh.*) But, I got many a young girl's telephone number. (*JACK pulls a deck of cards from his pocket.*) My favorite was —

ENZO. Jack. I really need to start getting ready.

JACK. Oh. Right. (*JACK slips the cards back into his pocket.*)

ENZO. If you could send someone with a key to open one of the lockers, I'd really appreciate it.

(*JACK is beginning to get irritated by Enzo's attitude.*)

JACK. (*Still smiling.*) Sure. (*Pause.*) I'd just like to say, it's a real privilege to be working with you. I'm proud that the —

ENZO. (*Cutting him off.*) Thanks, Jack. But we're not gonna have any show, if I don't start gettin' ready.

(*Beat.*)

JACK. Right.

(*JACK extends his hand to ENZO, who reluctantly shakes it.*)

JACK. And I'm sure it's gonna be a great show. (*JACK exits. After a few beats, HE bursts back into the room.*) If you think of anything else you need, anything at all, just tell a busboy that *Jack* said it was okay. (*JACK pulls a card out of his deck to punctuate his words. Unfortunately, the card that HE has pulled is not a jack. Embarrassed, HE exits, mumbling to himself.*)

ENZO. (*Looking around the room.*) Jesus, what a dump.

(HE checks his watch. After a beat, HE starts toward his garment bag, then sees his reflection in the mirror. HE stops and takes a long look at his face.
HE walks over to the tape player and hits the "play" button.
An aria from "The Marriage of Figaro" begins to play.
ENZO listens to the music for a beat. We see his body relax. HE takes a deep breath, then grabs his garment bag and carries it into the bathroom.
After a few beats, the door to the hallway opens and MARION KELLY, an attractive woman in her 40's, dressed in an evening gown, stands in the doorway. Her face is flushed.
SHE is holding a wine glass and a bottle of champagne in one hand and a purse and an expensive looking coat in the other. SHE looks about the room. Thinking that SHE is alone, MARION slowly enters and closes the door behind her. SHE flops down in a chair and pours herself a glass of wine, then stares off into space. SHE listens to the opera music for a beat, then turns it off.
ENZO, now wearing a turban and a brocaded tuxedo jacket, comes out of the bathroom.
MARION and ENZO stare at each other. It's hard to tell who is more shocked.)

ENZO. Hello.
MARION. Uh ... Hello.

(Beat.)

ENZO. *(Smiling.)* You kinda startled me.

(MARION doesn't respond.
SHE notices that SHE is still holding the wine bottle and attempts to look composed as SHE hides it behind her back.)

ENZO. You okay?
MARION. If you're ... finished ... could you please leave?
ENZO. Leave?

MARION. (*Curt.*) Yes.

ENZO. Is something the matter?

MARION. No. Are you a meat wholesaler?

ENZO. You know many meat wholesalers who wear turbans? (*HE points to the suitcase.*) I'm tonight's entertainment. (*With bravado.*) Pasquini The Magnificent. I'm gettin' ready.

(*ENZO waits for MARION to tell him what she is doing in the room. SHE just stares at him.*)

MARION. (*Snapping.*) Mr. ...

ENZO. Pasquini.

MARION. Mr. Pasquini, the Ladies Room is jammed. The bar is a meat market. I need a quiet place to think for a few minutes. I'm sure that you can very easily find someplace else to get ready. (*MARION waits for Enzo to leave.*)

ENZO. (*Forcing a smile.*) I don't think you quite get the picture. I gotta make some magic in about a half hour. So, I'm not goin' anywhere.

(*MARION glares at Enzo, then notices the bathroom door. SHE quickly walks in and locks the door behind her.*
ENZO is left standing ... staring at the door. HE slowly walks over.)

ENZO. Hey ... Yoo hoo ... HEY! (*Beat.*) What the hell do you think you're doin'?! I got my stuff in there! (*Beat.*) HEY! Fine. We'll just let Jack sort this out. (*HE starts for the door that leads to the restaurant. After a beat, the bathroom door flies open.*)

MARION. Stop! I said stop! Jack Thomas gets most of his business from my husband's company. If you're interested in keeping this job, I suggest that you stay where you are and keep your *mouth shut.*

ENZO. Alright, that's it. End of conversation! C'mon. Let's go for a little walk.

(*As ENZO approaches her, MARION raises the wine bottle.*)

MARION. You touch me and I'll hit you over the head with this bottle!

(ENZO struggles with MARION and finally yanks the bottle away from her.)

ENZO. I need this job and I'm not gonna let you screw it up. *(HE grabs her arm.)*
MARION. Stop it! Let go of me! I'll scream!
ENZO. Go ahead! *(ENZO starts to lead her out of the room.)*
MARION. I'll tell Jack!
ENZO. Screw Jack! *(ENZO continues to lead MARION toward the door.)*
MARION. I can't go! Listen to me!
ENZO. No!
MARION.Listen! *(Blurting it out.)* I just punched my husband in the face!

(It takes a moment before this registers with Enzo. HE stops pushing MARION toward the door. THEY both stare at each other.
ENZO is not quite sure what to say. HE lets go of Marion's arm and puts the bottle down on the table.)

ENZO. You punched him?

(MARION sits down.)

ENZO. Why?
MARION. Just ... shut up.
ENZO. Is he lookin' for you? *(Beat.)* Hey, you can't tell me you cold cocked your husband, then just drop it!
MARION. Yes, I can.
ENZO. I got enough problems. I don't need a domestic squabble back here.
MARION. If you're afraid, leave.

ENZO. You're the one that should leave!

(Angry, MARION opens her purse. SHE begins to search through it. Nearly hysterical, SHE pours the contents out on the table: a wallet, a brush, a compact, lipstick, a Kleenex packet and breath mints.
ENZO can't help but watch her.)

MARION. (*Looking through the wallet.*) Perfect. No money, no credit cards, no keys ... The story of my life. Always prepared.

(MARION notices ENZO watching her. In an attempt to look nonchalant, SHE puts a mint in her mouth, then quickly throws everything back into the purse.)

ENZO. You need a couple of bucks for cab fare?
MARION. No thank you.

(There is an awkward silence.)

ENZO. Alright. Stay until you calm down. But don't move. Don't talk. And don't look at me.

(MARION closes her eyes. ENZO turns the tape player on again, then walks to the mirror and attempts to button his shirt collar.
LOUD THUNDER is heard offstage.
The thunder startles MARION. SHE notices ENZO struggling with his collar.
SHE tries to ignore him. As HE fusses with the collar, SHE realizes that HE is having trouble with his fingers.
ENZO sees her watching him.)

ENZO. What did I say? You're lookin' at me!

(MARION looks away. HE finally gets the collar buttoned, then pulls a black bow tie out of his pocket. HE places it around his neck and slowly tries to tie it. His fingers are stiff and clumsy.

HE tries to hide his awkwardness from Marion as HE continues to fumble with the tie.)

ENZO. (*Mumbling to himself.*) Goddamn it. Why the hell do they make these things impossible to ... Stupid little ...

(As HE works with the tie, HE continues to mumble obscenities to himself. MARION can't help but see and hear him struggling. At first SHE tries to ignore him, but it's impossible.)

MARION. (*Hesitating.*) Cross the back one over and then through.

(ENZO ignores her.)

MARION. Over ... Then through.
ENZO. (*Irritated.*) I told ya not to talk. I can tie it!
MARION. Fine.
ENZO. I can!
MARION. I said, fine!
ENZO. I can tell by your "fine," that you don't believe me!
MARION. You're also a mind reader?
ENZO. You don't need to read minds to get your meaning.
MARION. Okay. Let's see you. (*SHE stops the tape player.*) C'mon ... tie it!

(ENZO looks at her for a beat. HE thinks about trying to do it, then humiliated, turns away and opens his suitcase.)

MARION. Too lazy to learn and too vain to admit it.
ENZO. (*Looking at her.*) Boy, you're something else. Your husband's got money, so everybody's supposed to jump when you talk.
MARION. That's right. Unfortunately, Mr. Pasquini, *men* only pay attention to women when sex or *money* is involved.
ENZO. Not when they have more to offer.
MARION. They never listen long enough to find out.

ENZO. Maybe if you did something, people would pay more attention to you?

MARION. (*Stung by this remark.*) I do lots of things. (*SHE takes a sip of wine.*)

ENZO. I'm sure you do. Your nails, your hair —

MARION. I'm a teacher!

ENZO. Really? Where? School For The Terminally Rude?

MARION. Swarthmore Junior College.

ENZO. Oh, yeah? Well ... (*HE can't think of a snappy retort.*) Good for you.

MARION. Yes, it is.

(*THEY both make a major show of ignoring each other. ENZO pulls a small colorful box out of the case and turns his back to Marion. When HE is sure that SHE isn't watching him, HE tries to open the "secret" door on the box. HE fumbles with the latch.*)

ENZO. (*Mumbling to himself.*) Jesus Christ ... You did this a hundred times at home ... (*HE tries again to manipulate the small latch with his left hand. HE fumbles with it and finally flings the box into the case. HE glares at Marion, then stands perfectly still, as HE tries to calm down. Slowly, HE begins to look through his case. HE pulls a rubber ball out and starts to nervously squeeze it with his left hand.*)

(*MARION looks up and sees the ball in Enzo's hand. HE puts the ball down and goes back to his props. As HE looks at Marion, for the first time, THEY see the sadness and desperation in each other's eyes.*)

ENZO. Uh ... I'm a little off, 'cause I ... I always get ready alone. (*Beat.*) So ... Just be quiet, okay?

(*MARION nods. ENZO pulls a silver dollar out of his pocket and begins to work it through his fingers.*
MARION is quickly lost in thought.)

AS ENZO continues to work the coin, HE begins to pace around the room. HE checks his watch.)

ENZO. (*To himself.*) Boy, these people eat slow. (*HE begins to vocalize ... grunts, squeaks, over annunciating words.*)

MARION. Could you please ... sit down.
ENZO. No.

(MARION walks to the emergency exit and opens it. Offstage the sound of POURING RAIN is heard. SHE walks back to the table and begins to pace.
ENZO takes three playing cards out of his jacket pocket. HE examines them, then places them face down on the top of his case. HE begins to play "Three Card Monty." After a few beats HE looks at Marion.)

ENZO. Where's the ace?

(MARION ignores him.
HE shuffles the cards again.
ENZO lifts up one of the cards, it's the ace. HE shuffles the cards again.)

ENZO. Where's the ace? Bet you can't find it. C'mon, afraid I'll make you look bad?
MARION. If I find it, will you shut up?
ENZO. If you don't, will you go?

(MARION just stares at him, as ENZO shuffles the cards again. SHE watches him closely, hesitates, then picks a card. SHE has found the ace.)

ENZO. Just go talk to him!
MARION. Why are you doing this?!
ENZO. What?
MARION. Badgering me. Can't you see I'm upset?!

ENZO. So am I!
MARION. Leave me alone!
ENZO. I was here first!

(Even ENZO realizes that HE sounds very childish.
MARION empties the bottle into her glass. SHE chugs down the
wine and stands.)

MARION. Good luck, tonight.

(MARION starts to gather up her things.
LOUD THUNDER is heard offstage.)

ENZO. What're you going to do?

(MARION continues to gather up her things.)

ENZO. I said you could stay 'til you calmed down.
MARION. That might be a couple of years. (*SHE starts for the*
door, then looks down at the bottle and stops.) Maybe I'll just wait
'til he's finished with dinner. (*SHE slowly walks back to the chair.*)
Why does my life always seem like a scene from a bad movie?
(*MARION tries to go back to her own thoughts.*)
ENZO. I don't know. I never went to the movies much. (*Beat.*)
Nobody's hair gets messed up. You notice that?
MARION. What?
ENZO. In the movies ... when they have sex. Whenever I had
sex, my hair got messed up.
MARION. Oh. (*Pause.*) Probably because most people don't
want real.
ENZO. No?
MARION. No.
ENZO. Real isn't always bad.
MARION. Said the man who makes illusions.
ENZO. Right. Well, like I said, I never went to the movies
much.
MARION. It's not just the movies. Do you know how

Shakespeare referred to sex?

ENZO. No.

MARION. "The beast with two backs." Sounds pretty interesting, doesn't it?

ENZO. (*A little embarrassed.*) Yeah ... And they're always young! You notice that?

MARION. With very neat hair.

ENZO. Exactly! Patty used to say, she could teach those young punks a thing or two about —

(Embarrassed, ENZO turns away. HE tries to tie his tie. HE finally gives up.
There is a silence.)

ENZO. My wife used to do it for me.

MARION. Oh.

(Neither of THEM looks at each other.)

ENZO. She traveled with me a lot. Thirty-one years.

MARION. Long time.

ENZO. Yeah. (*Pause.*) You got kids?

MARION. Why?

ENZO. Just curious. Might be a reason to try and patch things up?

MARION. They're all grown up now.

ENZO. Sure. (*ENZO laughs softly to himself.*) When you started yellin' at me, you kinda reminded me of her.

MARION. Your wife? Why?

ENZO. She was Irish. She had a mouth on her. (*HE pulls out his wallet and shows her a picture.*)

MARION. Very pretty.

ENZO. Yeah, she was.

(THEY look at each other, there is an awkward moment. ENZO slowly puts his wallet away. MARION hesitates, then reaches into her purse and pulls out her wallet. SHE opens it and shows

Enzo a picture.)

ENZO. Two boys. Good looking.
MARION. Thank you.
ENZO. We never had any kids.
MARION. Oh.
MARION. (*Smiling.*) I'm Irish, too.
ENZO. I knew it!
MARION. O'Reilly.
ENZO. Of course, you're much more refined than Patty was. Her father brought her over from the old country when she was a girl. She started workin' when she was only ten. Never had much education.

(MARION smiles.)

ENZO. I know what you're thinkin'. Who am I talkin' about her lack of education?
MARION. No. Actually, I was thinking of something else, totally.
ENZO. What?
MARION. My being refined.

(THEY look at each other.)

ENZO. You are. You're kind of a pain in the ass but I can tell.
MARION. Years of pretending.
ENZO. No, you can't fake that.

(Beat.)

MARION. My father owned a bakery.
ENZO. No foolin'?
MARION. I can still make a lemon meringue pie that would take your breath away.
ENZO. How'd you hook up with "Mr. Veal Cutlets"?
MARION. He was lost. He came into the bakery for directions.

It wasn't in the best neighborhood and he was sort of nervous and scared. I thought he was the most — (*MARION stops, then turns away. SHE tries not to cry, but the tears begin to roll down her cheeks. SHE attempts desperately to stop the tears and compose herself. SHE begins to sob.*) I told him I was leaving him and he laughed at me. It was like he knew, I'd pick up my coat and start for the door, but ... He didn't even have the courtesy to lie this time. He always lied before.

(*ENZO looks at her. HE doesn't know what to do. After a long moment, HE slowly walks over and sits next to her. HE awkwardly puts his arms around her. SHE pulls away at first but then buries her face in his shoulder and sobs.*)

MARION. (*Crying very hard.*) She's the quality control expert at the plant. She's twenty-four years old. Her name is *Heather!* (*SHE looks at Enzo.*) She came over to our table ... She called him Michael ... I knew. (*Sobbing again.*) How can I compete with a twenty-four year old, named *Heather?* My children grew up. My husband got bored with me. When did this all happen?

(*HE strokes her face, trying to console her. Impulsively, HE kisses her gently on the cheek.*
MARION suddenly clings to him passionately. Instinctively, ENZO returns the embrace.
After a few beats, embarrassed, MARION pulls away.
Beat.
SHE dries her tears.)

MARION. I'm very sorry.
ENZO. (*A little embarrassed.*) No problem. (*Pause.*) I hope you don't think I was gettin' fresh?
MARION. No.

(*THEY look at each other.*)

MARION. Well ...

ENZO. Well ...

MARION. This is one of those moments, when it would be very helpful if a huge hole opened up, so I could jump in.

ENZO. C'mon ... Nothin's that bad.

(SHE stands and starts to gather up her things.)

ENZO. Uh ... I knew this guy. He was pretty old.

(SHE grabs her purse. ENZO is sitting on her coat.)

MARION. *(Trying to politely cut him off.)* I need my ...

ENZO. Oh, sure.

(ENZO stands awkwardly and MARION grabs her coat.)

MARION. Very nice meeting you.

ENZO. You, too. *(Pause.)* This guy's wife died. So he —

MARION. Well, I guess I'll be ... I'll see you.

ENZO. Okay.

(MARION starts for the door.)

ENZO. He was like suicidal.

MARION. *(Stops but doesn't look back at Enzo.)* This guy you knew?

ENZO. Right.

MARION. And what did ... this guy do?

ENZO. He took up hang gliding.

(Beat. SHE turns.)

MARION. What?

ENZO. He took up hang gliding.

MARION. You hang glide?

ENZO. No. This guy I know does. Everybody figured he did it so he could kill himself. Well, guess what? He started to win all of

these contests. Now he's like a big shot in the national hang
gliding society.

(MARION is a little confused.)

ENZO. Don't you get it?
MARION. No.
ENZO. He was still alive. He just had to prove it to himself.
MARION. Goodbye.

(MARION starts to leave.
HE grabs HER arm.)

ENZO. Wait a minute.
MARION. That's the second time you've grabbed me!
ENZO. *(Letting go of her arm.)* What are you gonna do?
MARION. That's none of your business. Why do you even
care?
ENZO. I don't know. *(ENZO stares at her for a beat.)*
MARION. I don't think we should discuss this anymore.
ENZO. Why? I don't even know your name.
MARION. Mrs. Michael Kelly. I thought you needed to
concentrate on getting ready?
ENZO. I do.
MARION. I'm a big girl. I can take care of myself.
ENZO. You sure?
MARION. Yes.
ENZO. You just gonna go back and kiss his ass?
MARION. I've been married twenty-one years! I'm a
professional housewife! Kissing his ass is what I do.
ENZO. What about your job?
MARION. *My job*? I volunteer one night a week for adult
classes. I teach bored housewives and retired auto mechanics to
draw.
ENZO. Boy, I gotta tell you, it's very hard to listen to you feel
sorry for yourself.
MARION. I don't recall asking you to listen!

ENZO. Don't get pissed off, but —

MARION. It's so easy for you to be judgmental, isn't it?!

ENZO. Not as easy as it is for you to roll over and play dead.

MARION. You have a *skill*! You can *do something*!!! You're not a *woman*!!

ENZO.What does that have to do with anything?!

MARION. It has everything to do with it! Why don't I just stand up for myself?! Why don't I leave my husband?! Well, it's not so easy, buster!!! I've —

ENZO. I haven't performed in two years! You think this is easy?!!!

MARION. I don't know!

ENZO. Let me tell ya, it's not! Life doesn't have shit to do with being a man or a woman! Nothin's easy!

(THEY stare at each other. ENZO suddenly embarrassed by his speech, goes back to his suitcase.)

ENZO. Like you said, it's none of my business.

(There is a long silence. ENZO picks up the ball and begins to squeeze it.)

MARION. Did you have a stroke?

ENZO. Is it that obvious?

MARION. No. I'm sorry. I didn't mean to embarrass you. My mother had one. I helped take care of her.

(Beat.)

ENZO. Did she recover?

MARION. Uh ... Strokes are all different.

ENZO. Yeah. That's right. *(HE checks his watch, then continues to squeeze the ball.)* I should probably warm up a little more.

MARION. Right. Good luck.

ENZO. You, too.

(ENZO goes back to looking at his props. MARION turns and heads for the door.)

ENZO. *(Without looking up.)* Try doin' something for yourself.

(MARION stops but doesn't look back at Enzo.)

ENZO. Like drawin'.
MARION. I'm not very good.
ENZO. Because Michael says so?
MARION. *(Turns and looks at him.)* No. Because I say so. *(Beat.)* He built a whole studio for me.
ENZO. Really? What happened?

(Beat.)

MARION. *(With difficulty.)* About a month after the studio was finished, I found out he had an affair with the contractor's secretary.

*(There is a long silence.
Neither knows what to say.)*

MARION. Such is life. *(With a sad smile.)* Beats working in a bakery. *(Pause.)* Bye. *(MARION grabs her purse, the bottle and the glass. SHE slowly walks off.)*

(ENZO looks at the case, then down at the ball in his hand. HE picks up "Pandora's Box" and stares at it for a long beat. HE holds it out in front of him.)

ENZO. *(Performing.)* Ladies and gentlemen ... Pandora's Box. This tiny cube can change your life! *(HE tries to manipulate the "secret latch.")* The mysteries of the ages wrapped up in this square! *(HE continues to fumble with the latch. HE is about to slam the box down, then HE stops and places it gently back in the*

*case. Finally, HE closes the suitcase and begins to latch it. LOUD
THUNDER is heard offstage. ENZO listens as HEAVY RAIN
begins to fall. HE stares at his reflection in the mirror. Beat.)*
Everything has to end sometime. Such is life.

*(ENZO grabs his suitcase and garment bag and starts for the door
that leads to the restaurant.
HE stops, then turns and heads for the emergency exit, just as
MARION walks back into the room.)*

MARION. Marion.

(Startled, ENZO looks at her.)

MARION. My name is Marion.
ENZO. Uh ... I'm Enzo.

(MARION notices that Enzo is leaving.)

MARION. Did they call for you?
ENZO. No. Not yet. *(With great difficulty.)* I was dynamite in
my living room. But here ...

(MARION just stares at him.)

ENZO. So, I guess I'll see you around. *(HE starts for the door.)*
MARION. You're not going to perform?

(ENZO shakes his head "no.")

MARION. This is hysterical. I was out in the hall getting really
mad at myself. I thought, here's this brave man, willing to carry on
after having a stroke. I was coming in to get a few words of ...
inspiration. *(SHE laughs softly to herself.)*
ENZO. I never said I was a role model. Look, I still wanna do
it. Performing is all I know! I've been makin' magic for forty
years! But now ... You saw. I'm not gonna make a fool of myself. I

deserve a little dignity.

MARION. (*Snapping.*) You don't owe me any explanation.

ENZO. That's right. (*ENZO starts to exit.*)

(*MARION notices a few props that have fallen on the floor. Beat.*)

MARION. You forgot something.

(*SHE picks up a deck of cards and a small notebook. SHE looks at the cards before SHE hands them to ENZO.*)

ENZO. Thanks.

MARION. Card tricks?

ENZO. Right.

(*SHE looks at him.*)

ENZO. I don't do card tricks. You want card tricks, ask Jack.

MARION. No thanks. (*MARION looks very sad and defeated.*)

ENZO. Jesus, it's not bad enough you got me all screwed up tonight, now you're gonna make me feel guilty!

(*Pause.*)

MARION. I'm sorry.

ENZO. You really want a card trick?

(*THEY look at each other.*)

ENZO. Okay. I'll try one. Then I gotta go. (*ENZO opens the deck of cards. Very serious.*) Aw, Geeze! I shoulda thrown these out! They're blank! (*HE fans the cards, they are white on both sides.*) Wait a second. I think there was a magic word that could make the cards turn back to normal. (*HE closes up the fan, then looks at Marion.*) It's been so long, I forgot what it was. Let's see. Was it presto? No. How 'bout ... Marion? (*ENZO looks at the* cards.) "Marion." (*Pause.*) Well, whatdya know? (*HE fans out the card. It's now a complete deck. HE flips the cards over. The backs are still white.*) Hmmmm. I told ya I was a little rusty. I got the faces, but not the backs. Maybe if I just rub 'em? I can heat 'em up ... and the backs will come back? (*ENZO takes the deck and rubs it on the table. HE then fans out the cards. They now have faces and backs.*)

MARION. Bravo !

ENZO. Something's still wrong with this deck. It just doesn't feel right. (*HE reforms the deck, then fans the cards again. They are white on both sides!*) How the hell did that happen?

(*MARION smiles and applauds.*

ENZO attempts to go on with the trick and suddenly fumbles the card, nearly dropping the entire deck. HE tries to recover.

MARION continues to smile, pretending that SHE didn't notice the glitch.

The performer in Enzo begins to emerge in spite of himself. HE places the case on the table, opens it and grabs another deck of cards.

HE opens the deck and fans the cards out in front of him.)

ENZO. Ladies and gentlemen. A tiny bit of prestidigitation for your viewing enjoyment. These particular cards were very expensive because they have a mind of their own! (*HE now attempts the "mental deck" card trick; a rather complicated manipulation. HE has a few problems, but executes the finish perfectly.*)

MARION. Wonderful!
ENZO. Not bad.
MARION. Do one more?

(*Beat.*)

ENZO. Sit down.
MARION. Why?

ENZO. Just sit down.

(HE walks over to the tape player and fast forwards the tape. HE stops it and hits "play." Magician "show music" is heard.
ENZO slips on his turban and pulls Pandora's Box out of the case.)

ENZO. (*Performing.*) Behold, the mystery of the ages. Pandora's Box! This tiny little cube can change your life! Madame, would you mind assisting me?
MARION. (*Making a big show of looking around.*) Me?
ENZO. Please, don't be shy. The spirits in the box will be kind, to so beautiful an assistant as yourself.

(MARION blushes. ENZO helps her to her feet, then picks up her purse.)

ENZO. Please hold your purse in one hand, like so. (*HE hands the purse to her.*) Hold it out in front of you.

(SHE does.)

ENZO. Now ... (*HE walks over to the case, picks up Pandora's Box, then pulls out a scarf. Very slowly and dramatically HE walks behind Marion and stops.*) Take Pandora ! (*HE hands the box to MARION.*) Hold it out in front of you.

(SHE does as instructed.)

ENZO. (*Performing to the audience.*) Without ever touching the box with my hands, I will make your most precious possession *transmutate* in your purse and then reassemble itself within the confines of Pandora's Box! May I have quiet, please! (*ENZO looks at Marion's purse.*) You're sure you have a good grip on it?
MARION. (*Fighting back a smile.*) Yes, I do.
ENZO. Good. I've seen objects thrown hundreds of feet into the air. (*ENZO stares at Marion.*) Ready?

MARION. I think so.

ENZO. Pandora commands you to ... *Transmutate!* (*HE runs the scarf over the purse. After a beat HE removes the scarf and stares at Marion. HE takes a deep breath and places the scarf over the box. Beat.*) Now ... Come to Pandora! (*HE whips the scarf away.*) Open the box!

MARION. Aren't you even going to say abracadabra?

ENZO. Pasquini The Magnificent commands you to ... open the box!

(*There is KNOCK at the door and JACK enters. HE is carrying a drink and looks a little drunk. HE has a large lipstick smudge on his cheek.*)

JACK. Mr. Pasquini, we're just about ready for — (*HE sees Marion.*) Mrs. Kelly? What are you doing here?

MARION. I took a wrong turn looking for the bathroom.

JACK. The Ladies Room is right next to the bar.

MARION. Really? Silly me ...

(*ENZO crosses to the tape machine and turns it off.*)

JACK. Shame on you.

MARION. What?

JACK. You missed dinner.

MARION. Uh ... I wasn't very hungry.

JACK. (*To Enzo, joking.*) Wife of a meat distributor and she passes up a beautiful piece of beef ... *center cut*, 3.98 a pound, wholesale! Not setting a very good example, I'd say. (*Back to Marion, smiling.*) Next thing you know, you'll say you've become a vegetarian. (*Still smiling.*) We all wondered what happened to you?

MARION. Well, now I guess you know.

JACK. Right.

(*There is a silence.*)

JACK. So, give me one moment and it will be my great pleasure to escort you back to your table. (*To Enzo.*) We're almost ready for you. There's a small elevated platform for you to work on. I had the bus boy put a table on it. You can use that for your props. I'll do your intro, then I'll cue your music. Don't take too long to set up.

(*ENZO just nods.*)

JACK. As they say in show business ... "Break a leg." (*JACK extends his arm to Marion, to escort her out of the room.*) Mrs. Kelly ...

(*MARION does not react.*)

JACK. If you're ready?
MARION. Uh ... Well ... I'll tell you, Jack. Since I'm here now, I think I'll just use this bathroom.

(*ENZO is surprised by this response. HE looks at Marion.*)

JACK. Are you sure?
MARION. A bathroom's a bathroom.
JACK. (*Hesitating.*) Alright. (*HE glances warily at Enzo.*) I'll wait for you.
MARION. Uh, it might be a while, if you get my drift?
JACK. Oh. You're sure you'll be okay?
MARION. I've been going to the bathroom by myself for quite a few years, Jack. I'm sure I'll be fine. (*MARION walks into the bathroom and closes the door.*)
JACK. (*Under his breath.*) What's going on here?
ENZO. Nothin'. She had a problem ... with her contact lens. Then I did a trick for her.
JACK. She made quite a scene a few minutes ago.
ENZO. No shit?
JACK. A major altercation with her husband.

(ENZO nods.)

JACK. (*Sotto voce.*) If she has more trouble with her lenses, I'd suggest you tell her to see an optometrist.

ENZO. I'll do that.

JACK. Your agent came.

ENZO. He did?

JACK. I put him at an empty table down in front. (*JACK checks himself out in the mirror. HE notices the lipstick smudge and quickly wipes it off.*)

ENZO. Jack ...

JACK. What?

ENZO. I …

JACK. Is there a problem?

ENZO. I know you're counting on me.

JACK. I certainly am. (*Pause.*) What?

ENZO. I don't —

JACK. Don't tell me you're not ready?

(Before ENZO can speak, MARION bursts out of the bathroom. SHE still has the box in her hand.)

MARION. (*Waving the box at Jack.*) Guess what's in it?

JACK. I have no idea!

(SHE opens it. Her breath mints are inside.)

MARION. My breath mints! I'm not sure it's my most prized possession, but it'll do.

JACK. (*Even more confused. Forcing a smile.*) What's going on?

MARION. Mr. Pasquini did the most wonderful trick for me.

JACK. Oh.

(ENZO and MARION look at each other.)

ENZO. You know how magicians are, Jack? Can't resist a

pretty face.

(MARION blushes.)

JACK. *(Trying to get back to business.)* So, what were you trying to say before?

MARION. He was trying to tell you that I've been bothering him!

JACK. You?

ENZO. No, that's —

MARION. Yes. But you can't blame me. He's been doing the most wonderful illusions for me!

JACK. Really?

MARION. Absolutely.

JACK. That's the kind of talk I like to hear. *(Conspiratorially, to Enzo.)* And the kind that'll make me entertainment chairman next year. They can't stop a couple of pros like us. *(JACK looks over at Marion.)* Are you ready to leave ... now?

MARION. Uh ... Actually, I got so excited about the trick ... I forgot to go. *(SHE hands the box back to JACK and hurries into the bathroom.)*

JACK. Is this Pandora's Box?

ENZO. Yes.

(JACK, ignoring Enzo, begins to examine the box.)

ENZO. Jack ... Look ... I know —

JACK. So ... How does it work?

ENZO. *(Takes the box from Jack and carefully places it in his case.)* Magic.

JACK. Magic?

ENZO. Absolutely.

(JACK is not sure what Enzo is talking about but HE tries to cover with a huge smile.)

JACK. Right. Magic.

(ENZO looks up at Jack, then snaps the case shut.
There is an awkward silence. Finally, JACK looks over to the
bathroom.)

JACK. This could take all night. (*Under his breath.*) Screw it.
Let her asshole husband come and get her. (*Beat.*) I'm counting on
you. (*Smiling.*) If you do well out there, I'm in as chairman. We
could work together a lot.

(The TWO MEN look at each other.)

ENZO. That's definitely something to think about.
JACK. You said it! I'll come and get you when we're ready.
(*Yelling at the bathroom.*) Lovely talking to you, Mrs. Kelly.
(*JACK waits for a response. None comes. HE shoots a look at*
Enzo, then walks out, mumbling to himself.)

(After a beat, MARION comes out of the bathroom.)

MARION. What a weasel.
ENZO. Why'd you tell him I was doing good?
MARION. Why'd you tell him I wear contact lenses?
ENZO. I was trying to protect your reputation.
MARION. I was trying to protect yours.

(Beat.)

ENZO. I can't do it anymore.
MARION. Are you forgetting you made my breath mints
transmutate?
ENZO. I also screwed it up two other times.
MARION. What about the card tricks?

(Beat.)

ENZO. Look, I ...

(THEY look at each other. ENZO realizes that MARION is counting on him.)

ENZO. I'm not givin' up. I'm just retiring. There's a difference. And even if I was givin' up ... That doesn't mean you have to.

MARION. I know. *(MARION picks up the deck of cards. SHE holds it out to him.)* The only time I've seen you smile, is when you were doing the card tricks.

ENZO. *(Taking the cards.)* You were very kind, but a beginner could do those. *(ENZO looks at Marion, then at the cards. HE walks back to his case.)*

MARION. I personally will be very disappointed.

ENZO. Sorry.

MARION. This is the first year I was looking forward to seeing the entertainment. *(SHE gently touches his hand.)* Please ...

(ENZO looks at Marion, then slowly opens his case. HE drops in the cards.

MARION nods. HE continues to look down at his props as SHE turns to leave.

HE looks up at her, then back to his props. HE pulls the "locking rings" out of the case.)

ENZO. *(To himself.)* The rings are a possibility, I guess.

(MARION stops and looks back at him.)

ENZO. Forget Three Card Monty. Miser's Dream is another possibility. I could probably use my right hand for the poke through pass with a cigarette ... If I use my right hand with the scarf pull ... Maybe I could do some simple tricks ... and finish with Pandora? *(HE looks at Marion.)* Is this really dumb?

MARION. I don't know.

ENZO. Well, I've been retired for two years. If I screw up, you can't get *more* retired. Maybe even a few of 'em will work?

MARION. I'm sure they will.

ENZO. Plus, if I really die out there, at least I'll have the pleasure of knowin' that Jack is goin' down in flames with me. *(ENZO smiles, then looks at his reflection in the mirror. HE notices that his tie is still undone. HE starts to fiddle with it, but still can't tie it.)* Goddamn it! This'll never —

(MARION comes over and ties it.
ENZO looks at the tie in the mirror. It's perfect. There is a real connection between them. Suddenly there is a KNOCK at the door.)

JACK. *(O.S.)* We're ready for you, Mr. Pasquini!
ENZO. Okay.
MARION. Good luck.
ENZO. I'll keep it simple. I'll keep it honest. And then I'll run like hell.

(MARION nods.)

ENZO. Besides, I'm not stupid enough to try hang gliding. *(Beat.)* What about you?

(THEY look at each other. MARION just shrugs.
There is a long silence.)

ENZO. Well ... "Into the Valley Of Death." *(ENZO starts to close up the suitcase.)*
MARION. *(Blurting.)* While I was in the bathroom ... Before I found the breath mints ... I was thinking ... Maybe ... I could ... give my sister a call? We're not very close. She doesn't really like me very much. But I could ... probably stay with her for a few days. They have a farm in Greensdale. They teach art students in their barn.
ENZO. Sounds nice.
MARION. It is.

(ENZO smiles.)

MARION. Well, I can't be worse off than I am now?

ENZO. *(Teasing.)* You never know.

MARION. *(Smiling.)* Right.

ENZO. Good luck to both of us. Maybe we could give each other a call? You know ... moral support.

MARION. *(Smiling softly.)* Next thing you know, our hair might get messed up. And then where would we be?

ENZO. *(A little embarrassed.)* I don't know?

MARION. Me, neither. Well, good bye.

ENZO. Bye.

MARION. *(Starts for the emergency exit, then stops.)* Uh ... Could I borrow some money?

ENZO. Sure. What d'ya need?

MARION. I don't know ... twenty?

ENZO. Take forty, you didn't have any dinner. *(ENZO gives her the money.)*

MARION. Thank you. Let me have your address ... so I can send you a check.

ENZO. Oh, right.

(ENZO slowly raises his hand, as if to stroke her cheek. HE "pulls" a business card from behind her ear. MARION giggles.)

MARION. Okay. *(Pause.)* This time I'm really leaving. *(MARION opens the door. SHE hesitates, then looks back at Enzo. SHE listens for a beat.)* Sounds like the rain stopped.

ENZO. That's good.

MARION. At least I won't get soaked.

ENZO. Things are lookin' up, already.

MARION. Right.

(THEY smile at each other.
MARION slowly exits.
After a beat, ENZO looks around the room one last time. HE notices that Marion has left her coat.

HE picks it up and starts after her, then stops. A smile forms on this face, as HE carefully hangs the coat, then places his garment bag over it.)

ENZO. Greensdale? (*Pause.*) Everybody needs a little magic. (*HE looks back at the coat, smiles, then grabbing his case, quickly hurries off. The LIGHTS FADE.*)

THE END

AUTHOR'S NOTE

The card manipulations referred to in the play should be kept simple. They should not slow the action down and they should also be basic enough, that the actor playing Enzo can learn them in one day.

I suggest the "Mirage Deck" and "Mental Photography."

Pre-rigged decks for these tricks can be purchased very inexpensively, at almost any joke or magic store.

If anyone working on the play wishes to substitute other manipulations, there are several very good books on card magic. I recommend, *The Art Of Magic,* by T. Nelson Downs and *Expert Card Technique*, by Jean Hugard and Fred Braue.

COSTUME PLOT

ENZO PASQUINI: raincoat, tuxedo, tuxedo shirt, black bow tie, white t-shirt, cape, turban

JACK THOMAS: tuxedo

MARION KELLY: evening gown, high heels, coat

PROPERTY PLOT

ENZO PASQUINI
suitcase (with "Pasquini The Magnificent" stenciled across the side)
umbrella
portable audio cassette deck
2 tape cassettes
small rubber ball
garment bag
Pandora's Box - a small, ornate wooden box, with a lid that opens and closes
three playing cards (one is an ace)
2 decks of trick playing cards
metal linking rings
large scarf
business card

MARION KELLY
champagne bottle
glass
purse
wallet
breath mints
photograph

JACK THOMAS
glass

piece of paper with notes written on it
wrist watch

SET DESIGN

The set can be very simple. A card table, a few chairs and perhaps a beat up sofa are the only furniture in the room. Stacked restaurant supplies, a mop, a trash can, fast food wrappers on the floor should give it a cluttered, disheveled appearance.

The only requirement is three exits. One leads to the offstage restaurant; one to the offstage bathroom and one is marked "Emergency Exit."

Sam Ingraffia

Sam Ingraffia has had plays produced in both New York and Los Angeles. Another one-act, *Chateau Rene*, was published by Samuel French as part of the 15th Annual Off-Off-Broadway Festival Series. Mr. Ingraffia is a member of the Dramatists Guild and the Alliance of Los Angeles Playwrights.

Other Publications For Your Interest

SIS BOOM BAA. Comedy. Sybil Rosen. 2m., 4f. Int. Football widows of America: This Is Your Life! Pam, Cheryl, Linda and Mary are best friends. They do everything together—because their husbands spend most of their time watching football on TV. Says Pam: "Compulsive football-watching is a male-reaction formation to the stress of being civilized. It's more bonding than Crazy Glue." Mary, the new-comer to the group has recently married Joey, and his obsession is really getting to her. While the women cook New Year's Day dinner in Cheryl's kitchen they coach Mary on technique—on how to get Joey's attention away from the game. We finally meet Joey when he comes into the kitchen for something to eat; and Mary tries what she has learned on him, to no avail—so she tackles him! **(#21681)**

FREEZE TAG. Comedy. Jacquelyn Reingold. 2f Ext. When Andrea tries to buy a newspaper in NYC's East Village, she is thrust onto an emotional journey she will never forget. Aldrich, the newsstand vendor, seems to know the most intimate secrets of Andrea's life, from childhood up to the present moment, including who her boyfriend is sleeping with and why. In this funny and touching play, two women are forced to confront who they are, who they once were, and what it means to be a friend. "Gripping and hilarious."—N.Y. Times. "Really terrific . . . one of the most impressive [playwriting] debuts of the season."—N.Y. Press. "An extraordinary play . . . an unforgettable experience."—Back Stage. **(#8678)**

LOOKIN' FOR A BETTER BERRY BUSH. Comic Drama. Jean Lenox Toddie (author of *Tell Me Another Story Sing Me a Song*, *A Scent of Honeysuckle* and *A Bag of Green Apples*). 2f. Ext. (simply suggested). Emma and Addie confront each other on the sidewalk of a city neighborhood. Emma is a proper woman who worked in a diner for forty years and "served more cups of coffee than you can count if you live to be a hundred." Addie, a street woman whose papa "set us t' wanderin' jes' a-lookin' fer a better berry bush," rummages in trash cans and sleeps in a cardboard box. This is the humorous and touching tale of two women, alienated from each other by vastly different life experience, who clash on a city street, only to find themselves sitting down together on a stoop in front of a brownstone, and tentatively reaching out for mutual understanding. **(#14927)**

Penguin Blues

by Ethan Phillips

Comic Drama. 1m., 1f. Int. This beautiful short play by actor Ethan Phillips of TV's "Benson" wowed them at Philadelphia Festival Theatre for New Plays. The critics were unanimous in their praise. We are in a room in an alcoholism rehabilitation center. The characters are Gordon, a manic alcoholic who knows the score, and Angelica, a nun who denies that she is an alcoholic. In the moving climax, Angelica finally recognizes why she is there; and in so doing, takes the painful first step towards sobriety. "One of the loveliest moments of emotional revelation I've seen in the theatre."—News of Delaware County.

(#18934)

Portfolio

by Tom Donaghy

Comedy. 1m., 1f., plus 1 offstage voice. Int. This amusing satire of advertising was produced to great audience mirth and critical approval at NYC's famed comedy theatre, Manhattan Punchline. We are on a photo shoot for a print ad campaign. The photographer, who is present only by voice, has had the brilliant idea to deck his model with live pigeons. He's hired a "pigeon man" to bring in a truckload of them. He becomes most annoyed, though, when the pigeons (which are mimed, by the way), won't take direction as easily as the model, much to the distress of the hapless pigeon man. Meanwhile, the model remains unflappable. In her business, she's used to anything and everything! (#18952)

Haiku

by Katherine Snodgrass

Drama. 3f., Int. This sublimely beautiful short play won the prestigious Heidemann Award given by the Actors Theatre of Louisville, perhaps the most important one-act play award in the United States. The story concerns a woman who lives with her retarded daughter, who has miraculously at brief intervals been "normal." In fact, the daughter, Louise, is sometimes super-normal, speaking in beautiful haiku poetry, which her mother has recorded and has had published under the mother's name. Then an older daughter, Billie, comes for a visit. Billie only knows her sister as hopelessly retarded, and refuses to believe that her mother's poetry has actually been composed by her sister. (#10650)

INCIDENT AT SAN BAJO
Drama
by Brad Korbesmeyer

3m., 4f. Bare Stage. The residents of a trailer camp at San Bajo have quite a story to tell, about a stranger who visited each one in turn, selling a mysterious elixir which he claimed would make them "live longer." Most of the residents of San Bajo did not buy the elixir of course—and they are now dead, the water supply having been poisoned by the mysterious stranger. Only seven are left to tell the tale—the seven who drank the elixir which, it turned out, was an antidote! Each tells his story in a series of interlocking monologues given to an unseen interviewer. The effect is somewhat like a "60 Minutes" segment, with an imaginary Morley Safer. This most unusual new play was the 1988 winner of Actors Theatre of Louisville's Heidemann Award, perhaps the most prestigious one-act play award in the United States.   (#11654)

BAIT AND SWITCH
Comedy
by Richard Dresser

3m., 2f. Int. Doug and Gary own and run a restaurant on the boardwalk which is fast going under, largely due to a recent influx of stinging jellyfish which has kept customers away from the beach, but also due to the fact that the two brothers are less than adept businessmen—particularly Gary, who isn't even aware that his brother is skimming profits. Their only hope is Kenny, a slick wiseguy with possible Mob connections. Kenny meets with Gary and Doug, sizes up the situation immediately, and eventually does take over the restaurant, forcing the two brothers out and, possibly, ending up with Gary's wife Lucy as part of the deal. Another incisive comic look at the American entrepreneurial mentality from the author of *The Downside, Better Days* and *Alone at the Beach*.   (#3948)

TONE CLUSTERS
Joyce Carol Oates
Drama

1m., 1f., plus 1 male voice. Bare stage. Frank and Emily Gulick are a nice middle-American couple with a nice house in a nice neighborhood. Why, then are they obviously under so much strain? As they are interviewed by an unseen interrogator, their story, and their predicament, emerges. The mutilated body of a 14 year-old girl from the neighborhood has been found in their basement, and their son is charged with the murder. Desperately, they cling to the belief that their son is not guilty, even as it becomes increasingly clear that he is the murderer. And, even as we are moved by the pitiable Gulicks, we ask ourselves, do they somehow share in the guilt of the crime? And: could we, as parents, someday find ourselves in their predicament? This extraordinary play by one of America's foremost women of letters won the prestigious Heideman Award bestowed by Actors Theatre of Louisville, which commissioned it and gave it its world premier at the famed Humana Festival. In *In Darkest America*.   (#22727)

THE ECLIPSE
Joyce Carol Oates
Drama

1m., 3f Int. Stephanie Washburn, a middle-aged college professor, lives with her mother Muriel in a small apartment in Philadelphia. Muriel was once a brilliant high school teacher. Now, she is retired, and her mind is going, possibly from Alzheimer's disease. As she goes in and out of reality, she makes her daughter's life miserable, even going so far as to call the local department of social services to accuse Stephanie of abusing her—a total fabrication, of course. Muriel also has a fantasy that she has a Latin lover, a Señor Rios, with whom she is carrying on a torrid affair. There is no Señor Rios, of course. Or is there? In the end, as flamenco music plays, Muriel enters, in a Spanish dancing dress, for her big date with Señor Rios, who appears, exactly as Muriel has described him, for a torrid dance with Muriel around the apartment as Stephanie sleeps in a chair, oblivious to it all. Then Muriel leaves for her date with the dark gentleman, and both women are finally released from their suffering. Death has finally claimed Muriel. This haunting play by one of America's foremost women of letters was commissioned by the Actors Theatre of Louisville, which produced it as part of their famed Humana Festival, and was subsequently produced Off Broadway in New York by Ensemble Studio Theatre. In *In Darkest America*.   (#7633)

Other Publications for Your Interest

NOW THERE'S JUST THE THREE OF US
(COMEDY)
By MICHAEL WELLER

4 men, 1 woman—Interior

Perry and Frank are roommates. Perry greatly envies Frank's expertise with the ladies, which he knows all about because Frank has told him. Well: enter one Deke. Neither Perry nor Frank knows Deke; but he convinces each that he is a good friend of the other and proceeds to move in. Deke is a *real* ladies' man. He brings his girlfriend in, too and they move into the bedroom, displacing Frank. When a mysterious man from ''the agency'' comes looking for Deke, he splits, leaving his girlfriend behind with Frank and Perry. She announces that she has decided to devote herself to sex, and Frank and Perry's eyes get bigger than saucers as they realize now, there's just the three of them! Premiered in London and has had many worldwide productions. An excellent choice for colleges by the author of *Moonchildren* and *Loose Ends*. (#16638)

THE TANGLED SNARL
(COMEDY)
By JOHN RUSTAN & FRANK SEMERANO

3 men, 2 women, 1 boy—Interior

To Private Detective Spuds Idaho, life in L.A. is ''. . . a 24 furlong race around a track made of quicksand.'' When the dying Legs Flamingo leaves him a package to deliver, Spuds gets curious. Why is Leslie Detweiler more interested in the package than in the death of her husband: ''Excuse me, but you look pretty collected for a lady whose breadwinner just got sliced four ways.'' Why was Legs mixed up with mob figure, Vito ''Fingers'' Scampi: ''So Fingers had Legs under his thumb.'' And how did it figure in with the Krieger heist: ''The Commissioner was embarrassed. His boys in blue were red in the face.'' With the aid of his secretary, Ginny, and a wise-cracking little kid, it all untangles for Spuds Idaho. (#22616)
